The Beauty of Holiness

A memoir unveiling spiritual intimacy

Sharon Longworth

The Beauty of Holiness
Published by Impressum, Newcastle NSW
© Sharon Longworth 2023
www.sharonlongworth.com
Cover and internal design by Impressum
www.impressum.com.au
Cover design by Emily Vergara

All rights reserved. No part of this publication may be reproduced, stored in, or introduced into a retrieval system, or transmitted, in any form, or by any means (electronic, mechanical, photocopying, recording or otherwise) without the prior written permission of the publisher.

National Library of Australia Cataloguing-in-Publication entry
Author: Longworth, Sharon
Title: The Beauty of Holiness / Sharon Longworth
ISBN: 978-1-922588-41-8 (print)
978-1-922588-42-5 (ebook)

Contents

Dedication vii
Preface ix
Acknowledgements xiii
Introduction xv

PART I
INFANCY IN CHRIST *1*

CHAPTER 1
Stagnation in the Aging Bride 3
The Power of Woman - An Instrument of Choice 11

CHAPTER 3
Snippets of My Story 15

CHAPTER 4
Not Flesh of My Flesh 24

CHAPTER 5
Enjoying the Milk but I Was Still Hungry 39

PART II
HEARING GOD'S VOICE *47*

CHAPTER 6
Learning to Hear God's Voice 49

PART III
SPIRITUAL GROWTH *79*

CHAPTER 7
My Battle with Depression 81

PART IV
SPIRITUAL MENU *105*

CHAPTER 8
The Blessing of Grace 107

CHAPTER 9
Apply the Butter to the Bread 116

CHAPTER 10
Place the Meat on the Altar 140

CHAPTER 11
Anyone for Vegetable 155

CHAPTER 12
Top it off with a Feast of Fruit Salad for Dessert 176

PART V
SPIRITUAL GIFTS *183*

CHAPTER 13
The Gift of Tongues 185

CHAPTER 14
The Gift of Prophecy 194

CHAPTER 15
The Gift of Healing 207

PART VI
SPIRITUAL RELATIONSHIPS *215*

CHAPTER 16
The Dowry of the Bride 217

CHAPTER 17
Three Equals One 248

CHAPTER 18
And the Two Shall Become One 261

CHAPTER 19
The Root of all Evil is Self 273

CHAPTER 20
It's all about Relationship 282

Chapter 21
The Heavenly Husband and His Latter Day Bride 289

Part VII
FINALLY 299

Chapter 22
The Wedding Vow - It's Your Choice.....................................301

REFERENCES 307

QUOTATIONS FROM SCRIPTURES..................................309

PART VIII
A COLLECTION OF SONG LYRICS AND POEMS 311

Lord, Give Me a Song..313
Take My Hand..315
What More Can I Say..317
Imagine 319
I Give You All the Praise 321
Just a Simple Song of Praise 322
Do You Know Him?..323
Freedom in Strife 325
A Mother's Heart for her Daughter...............................329
Our Beautiful Boy 332
My Beautiful Daddy...336
My Dad!..341

ABOUT THE AUTHOR 343

Dedication

I wish to dedicate this book to my beautiful Dad, Don McKeough, who passed away on the 1st of January, 2013. Your unswerving dedication and steadfast love for God is a lasting legacy that you and Mum have faithfully passed on to our family. For this, we are eternally grateful to you both. Your gift of love and faithfulness to God and your family will continue to live on in the pages of this book. We love you, Dad, and miss you more than words can say! We are so very much looking forward to seeing you again in Glory!

Preface

The Lord whispered the following words to me when I was seeking and sensing His leading concerning a new title for my story: *"Open your eyes to see the Beauty of Holiness; this is at the heart of your story and Mine. 'The Beauty of Holiness!'"*

Just as my life is a work in progress, so too has been the journey of this book. With the introduction of a new title, I ask the following questions: Will Jesus return to earth to find His Bride arrayed in 'The Beauty of Holiness?' Or will she be caught floundering and unprepared to meet her Bridegroom, suffering with symptoms of spiritual stagnation, a 'spiritual menopause', as it were? Will she be barren as a 'dry reed', her spiritual womb being non-productive and lacking in life-giving seed, hindering the flame and flow of Holy Spirit power in her life?

The concept of spiritual menopause originally came to me in a vision. I was in bed, drifting in and out of sleep, when I had very clearly seen in front of me the words:

MENOPAUSE AND THE LATTER-DAY BRIDE

'Where on earth did that come from?' was my immediate thought. In my bewilderment, I assumed this to be the title of a book. I later searched online, only to discover that no such book existed.

After considering this strange phenomenon for a time, a realisation occurred to me: 'Surely the Lord would not be suggesting that 'I' should write the book! I mean to say, I am just an over-the-hill country hairdresser with no clue or skills in writing an essay, let alone a book. My only qualification is in cutting hair. What would I know that could be of interest or benefit to anybody else? What has menopause got to do with the latter-day Bride, anyway?'

Yet, despite my protests, that almost annoying nudge and still small voice kept urging me on, saying, 'You can do it. Just write down your story.'

So here I am, entirely reliant on the Lord and His leading, eagerly waiting to see what ends up on the page.

You may ask yourself: 'Who on earth is the latter-day Bride?'

Well, the Bride refers to all God's chosen people who believe Jesus is the promised Messiah, as prophesied in the Old Testament and fulfilled in the New Testament.

The latter-day is the current time we live in, which is the end of the Church Age. The Church Age, also known as the Apostolic Age, commenced at the first coming of Jesus as a baby born in Bethlehem over 2000 years ago and will conclude when He returns to earth as the King of kings and Lord of lords. Just before His very public return, He will mysteriously retrieve His Bride to Himself in an event known in Christian circles as The Rapture.

The big question is, 'In what state will Jesus find you and me when it's time to meet our Heavenly Husband face to face? Will we be a glorious Bride? Not having spot or wrinkle or any such thing, but holy and without blemish, as Paul speaks of in Ephesians 5:27? Or will we be suffering from debilitating symptoms of 'spiritual menopause', stagnant in our fruitfulness and productivity as God's chosen Bride?

Acknowledgements

I wish to thank my very talented niece, Emily Vergara, for designing the cover of my book, incorporating her painting of the Spirit-filled Bride depicting the Tongues of Fire and the River of Life, who is the Holy Spirit. Through Holy Spirit Impressions, the Lord mysteriously and simultaneously showed me the original title and Emily the picture of the Bride for the cover. We finally put two and two together twelve months down the track, realising that the Lord had instigated the whole thing. He is amazing, and so are you, Emily! All your gifts and talents are so very much appreciated!

Thanks to those of my beautiful family members for being willing to have personal aspects of your lives exposed in the contents of this book. I love you all heaps!

Special thanks to my husband, Andrew, for your endless love, patience, and support while writing and revising my story. I am forever grateful that I have had you by my side in this journey of life.

To those of my many family members and friends who have stood by me and graciously tolerated the lengthy progression of this project, I say a huge thank you from the bottom of my heart! A special mention, especially to those of you who contributed with gentle nurture, encouragement and helpful suggestions as each edition unfolded. You know who you are!

Also, thank you so much to Sheree, Emma and the team at Impressum for your time and patience, practical help and skills in preparing this manuscript for re-publishing. Your expertise is so much appreciated! Thank you!

All praise, glory, and honour go to my Heavenly Husband Jesus, my Lord, my God, and my Saviour! Indeed, without Him, this book would never have come to fruition.

Contact the author: author.sharonlongworth@gmail.com

Introduction

The Beauty of Holiness is a narrative of my journey as I searched for more in my relationship with God, my Heavenly Father, also known as my Heavenly Husband. At the heart of my story is the Christian idea of spiritual marriage. Jesus is the Bridegroom and the Church, His followers, His Bride.

I had been a Christian for many years, knowing assurance of my salvation by God's grace. Yet, my relationship with my Heavenly Husband had become stagnant, causing me to feel unfulfiled, unproductive and lacking in power. I believed there was much more to experience as a child of the living God and as a chosen Bride of Christ. I wondered what was missing in my spiritual journey, causing me to feel less than I should be as a Christian.

It eventually became evident through a not-so-subtle hint from the Lord that I was suffering from *Spiritual Menopause*. A proverbial stagnancy and blockage in my growth as a Christian that kept me from being the holy Bride God intended me to be. I wonder whether you can relate to any of the following symptoms of this spiritually debilitating condition:

Temperature Fluctuations – There were times when I would be *on fire* for the Lord, knowing a close and warm sense of union with His Spirit. Then, without warning, usually due to life's circumstances, I felt as though I was out in the cold. My relationship with my Heavenly Husband had fizzled to a cold dying ember, leaving me with a sense of loss as though He had inadvertently removed me from His presence.

Restlessness – I could not *rest* in knowing that God loves me and knows my every need and oversees every aspect of my life. My inability to relax and to *rest in Him* left me grappling with worry, fear and anxiety. I lacked in knowing the abiding peace and presence of Jesus, instead feeling 'afflicted…, tossed with tempest, and not comforted' (Isaiah 54:11 NKJV).

Dulled Hearing – I was taught from a young age that the Holy Spirit would be my counsellor and guide. Yet, I did not know how to hear or recognise His voice. I could not determine His will for my life and what direction I should go. My life was like stagnant water in a blocked drain pipe, gurgling around looking for direction, unable to flow and confidently move forward.

INTRODUCTION

Depressed Spirit – For many years, I lived under the bondage of a *spirit of heaviness*, feeling downcast and defeated under a cloud of darkness. I was vulnerable to Satan's attack, and he delighted in keeping me bound in spiritual and physical bondage.

Complacency – Even though I would read my Bible regularly, I could not retain God's Word in my memory for very long. I *lacked discipline* in memorising scripture due to *complacency* and *laziness*. I could not confidently recall and speak out God's Word when faced with opposition and the enemy's lies.

Ill-defined Identity – Despite being a Christian for many years, a vague or poor understanding of my *true identity in Christ* left me ill-equipped and powerless to overcome life's struggles. I felt defeated and even burdened with guilt when faced with spiritual and fleshly battles.

Dormant Mind – A blocked mindset kept me from maturing and moving forward in my faith due to a slave-to-the-flesh mentality. I believed I could never be holy until I was promoted to heaven. I was weary and frustrated in my spiritual walk as I tended to rely on my fleshly nature for empowerment. I would strive in my own strength, rather than relying on the power of the Holy Spirit to transform me into the person God would have me be, which is pure and lovely, portraying 'The Beauty of Holiness'.

If you can relate to the above symptoms, I pray you will be encouraged to know that your condition can improve as you read my story. May you develop an unquenchable thirst and hunger to invest in your relationship with God, who is the Antidote and Salve for every symptom and wound we bear. May you have a burning desire to know and understand the mystery of Christ in you, empowering you to be the holy Bride for whom Jesus is returning to take to Himself! May you grow and mature from *infancy* in your spiritual growth and knowledge of your Heavenly Father to knowing *intimacy* with Him as your Heavenly Husband, once again flowing and growing by, and in, His Spirit.

PART I

Infancy in Christ

CHAPTER 1

Stagnation in the Aging Bride

> For your Maker is your husband, The LORD of hosts is His name; And your Redeemer is the Holy One of Israel; He is called the God of the whole earth (Isaiah 54:5 NKJV).

'For your Maker is your husband …!'

I don't know about you, but I find this concept to be a little strange. I was adopted into God's family as an infant child at age nine. I have always related to God as my loving Heavenly Father, not my loving Heavenly Husband. Yet, it was God who would initiate the marriage relationship between a man and a woman at the beginning of time, modelling for us an intimate bond that replicates the union between God the Father, God the Son, and God the Holy Spirit, being three separate persons, yet mysteriously One. God's design was that marriage would be an intimate union between a man and a woman, a bridegroom and a bride. This biblical and Christian idea of marriage forms the heart of my story.

My Heavenly Father has ordained it to be so that I, His adopted child, would also be known as His Bride, having a mysterious union with Him as my Heavenly Husband. This twofold relationship could only be morally acceptable between a sovereign God and His created being. You will discover in this book that, when referring to God, I interchange between calling Him my Heavenly Father *and* my Heavenly Husband simply because He is both.

As stated, God is three persons in One - God the Father, the Son, and the Holy Spirit. Just as in the natural, we are a baby when first born, so too, we are babies when we are spiritually reborn, relating as a child to God the Father, as our Heavenly Father. But as we mature, we relate more and more to God the Son, Jesus, as the lover of our soul, as our Heavenly Husband. God the Holy Spirit is our wise friend and counsellor.

God's Word tells us that the Lord Jesus will one day return to earth to present His Bride to Himself as a glorious Church, not having spot or wrinkle or any such thing but that she will be *holy and without blemish* (Ephesians 5:27 NKJV).

How wonderful it would be if a young bride could forever retain her youthful glow in the natural scheme of things. She would not be concerned with physical decline resulting in unbecoming spots, wrinkles, blemishes, etc. Sadly, the reality of a world falling from perfection becomes evident when a 'maturing bride' looks in the mirror. The years seemingly fly by, and without reasonable notice, she unsuspectingly finds herself approaching the 'other side of the hill,' so to speak. As she draws nearer to the latter years of her life, she will likely find herself having to contend with the many insidious symptoms of menopause, which align with the spiritually stagnant symptoms outlined in the introduction, noted here in brackets, such as those infamous hot flushes (*temperature fluctuations*), vagueness (*Ill-defined identity*), memory loss (*due to*) *complacency*), depression (*depressed spirit*), insomnia (*restlessness*) and fatigue (*dormant mind*), just to mention a few.

The changes in her body may cause her to feel as though she is emotionally, physically and mentally incapable of responding to the affections and intentions of her husband as she did when she was young and blossoming. It may seem like her blossom has withered as a 'dried up reed' (Isaiah 19:6-7 NKJV), causing her to feel unattractive and undesirable, leaving her with a sense of defeat and little use to her husband. She feels like a 'withered fig tree' (Matthew 21:19 NKJV), fearful of no longer being loved and desired.

As we consider the fears of the stagnant bride as she battles with physical and fleshly decline, I ask the question: How is it that a marriage relationship may be impacted by the onslaught of menopause, or stagnation in the aging bride, as it were?

What it all boils down to is this: The *desires* and *intent* of a loving husband are undermined and thwarted by his bride's *battle* with the *flesh*.

Does this sound familiar, by any chance? I am assuming others can relate to the above statement, whether it applies to your earthly marriage or your relationship with your Heavenly Husband. I am sure others have experienced the feeling of being defeated by the flesh. The feeling of inadequacy and failure when it comes to being the person God intended and designed us to be.

The aging bride struggles with the dilemma of longing to be a good wife in fulfilling her husband's desires and intentions toward her. However, she is sadly aware that she falls a long way short, being physically incapable of doing so.

For the sake of their marriage, she must find a solution. I believe we find the answer in Ephesians chapter 5:22-29, although be aware that some may initially misunderstand, or even refute, what Paul is suggesting here. But I urge you to remember that the relationship between husband and wife is represented here as being a counterpart of the relationship between Christ and His Bride, the Church.

> Wives, submit to your own husbands, as to the Lord. For the husband is head of the wife, as also Christ is head of the church;

and He is the Savior of the body. Therefore, just as the church is subject to Christ, so *let* the wives *be* to their own husbands in everything.

Husbands, love your wives, just as Christ also loved the church and gave Himself for her, that He might sanctify and cleanse her with the washing of water by the word, that He might present her to Himself a glorious church, not having spot or wrinkle or any such thing, but that she should be holy and without blemish. So husbands ought to love their own wives as their own bodies; he who loves his wife loves himself. For no one ever hated his own flesh, but nourishes and cherishes it, just as the Lord does the church (Ephesians 5: 25-29 NKJV).

According to God's instruction through the apostle Paul, it would *'seem'* (emphasis on seem) that the bride must choose to surrender her will to her husband's will. She must learn to practise *selfless submission* to her husband's desires and intentions toward her! She is to be subject to her husband's authority over her!

Ouch!

But wait! In case you are tempted to close the book in apparent indignation, have we really understood what the passage is saying?

The stagnant bride, both in the natural and the spiritual, is battling with her fleshly limitations, feeling unfulfilled and unproductive. She is anxious to please her husband and fulfil his desires, yet she lacks the ability to do so. At this point, it is imperative to acknowledge the husband's role, as Paul affirmed in the above passage. He is to love his aging bride unconditionally and selflessly. For the sake of his marriage, He *will not* demand from her more than she can easily and willingly give. A loving and submissive wife gives herself to her husband to the best of her ability. In turn, a loving husband acknowledges her limitations and puts his wife's needs before his own, willingly laying down his life in self-sacrifice for the sake of his aging and stagnant bride.

And so it is with our loving and adoring Heavenly Husband in His care for His spiritually stagnant Bride! He lays down His life in self-sacrifice out of unconditional love for her, knowing that she is incapable of being a perfect Bride in her fallen fleshly struggles and efforts.

Enter Holy Spirit power, who does His work in her of gentle sanctification. As the stagnant Bride submits to her Heavenly Husband's love and authority over her, becoming one with Him in Spirit, He slowly but surely transforms her into the pure and holy Bride He intended her to be.

Psalm 110:3 speaks of the last days of the Church age that we are currently living in, when God's people will serve Him willingly, being anointed with His Spirit in purity and power in readiness for the birthing of God's Kingdom on earth:

> Your people shall be volunteers In the day of Your power; In **the beauties of holiness**, from the womb of the morning, You have the dew of Your youth. (NKJV) [Emphasis mine]

'*In the beauties of holiness*' translates in Hebrew into 'the loveliness of a pure people'. '*From the womb of the morning*' literally means 'birthed into a new day'. '*You have the dew of your youth*' translates in Hebrew as 'the anointing of boyhood or girlhood', with an untainted anointing.

This passage gives me hope and assurance in the knowledge that a wonderful transformation will occur in a stagnant and powerless Bride. She will be anointed with renewed youthfulness, tainted no longer with spots, wrinkles and blemishes, willingly serving her Heavenly Husband as she submits to His authority and power. A submissive Bride is anointed with

Holy Spirit power, renewed and equipped to serve her Heavenly Husband as the new dawn of a new Kingdom ushers in.

Chapter 2

The Power of Woman - An Instrument of Choice

I am intrigued by the following:

At the end of chapters 26 & 27 in Genesis, the very first book of the Bible, there is a reference to Esau's two wives. Their names are Judith and Basemath. These two wives of Esau were Hittite women, and this upset his parents, Isaac and Rebekah. They experienced *grief* in both *mind* and *spirit* because of these two daughters-in-law. Rebekah even goes so far as to say, if her other son Jacob marries a woman such as these, that life will not be worth living.

There is no other mention of these two women anywhere else in these chapters. All we know is that Judith and Basemath caused Isaac and Rebekah to grieve in both *mind* and *spirit*. Besides the fact that they were pagan women, I am left wondering what else they may have done to cause such grief to their mother and father-in-law. They certainly had a massive impact on the lives of the people around them.

The apparent physical and spiritual grief and devastation brought upon this family due to *choices* that were made by Esau and his wives is typical of the adverse effect that *freewill* has had on all of humanity.

After reading about these two wives, I was reminded of another wife whose story is also told in Genesis. I am referring to Eve, the wife of Adam, the very first man and woman God created. As I was thinking about Eve, Judith and Basemath, and their significant influence on the people around them, the Lord impressed upon my mind the following words: Eve was an '*instrument* of *choice*'.

This statement is referring to Eve being instrumental in the fall of man from perfection. The choices she made altered the destiny of all of God's creation. It would seem that Eve dominated her husband as she succumbed to the influence of Satan. She overpowered Adam through persuasive means by convincing him to give in to his fleshly desires. Ultimately, they both chose to eat the fruit God had forbidden them to eat.

Their disobedience resulted in the breakdown of the relationship between them and their creator, God. For the first time in history, man and woman would know first-hand what it feels like to experience grief and devastation in both the physical and the spiritual realm.

In the perfect Garden of Eden, Adam and Eve had known an intimate one-on-one communion with their God. When Eve took matters into her own hands as an 'instrument of choice,' she succeeded in causing a major rift in the relationship between God and His creation, ultimately bringing about the downfall and destruction of all humanity. Their peaceful union they knew with God was severed, and they were separated from Him for eternity. God had given Adam specific instructions.

> And the Lord God commanded the man, "You are free to eat from any tree in the garden; but you must not eat from the tree of the knowledge of good and evil, for when you eat of it you will surely die" (Genesis 2:16-17 NIV).

Adam and Eve would die as a consequence of choosing to eat the fruit of the forbidden tree. Physical and eternal death was set in motion. Though they did not physically die immediately, they experienced immediate physical and spiritual separation from God. They were both banished from His presence. They were cast out of the Garden of Eden and prohibited from re-entering.

As an added consequence of Adam and Eve's actions, every human being who comes into the world is born physically alive but spiritually separated from God. His purpose and intent of knowing *spiritual intimacy* with His creation were thwarted due to Eve succumbing to her fleshly desires and the deceitful tempting of Satan.

How different things may have turned out for the whole of humanity if Eve had exercised selfless submission and obedience to instruction. If only she had been subject to the authority and command of God. If only she had surrendered to His will, putting His desires and intent before her own.

Yes, that dreaded word *submission* keeps coming up, but more about that later. Allow me to tell you some more of my story.

CHAPTER 3

Snippets of My Story

When I was young, I used to wear long socks to hide my skinny legs!

Yes, you read that correctly the first time, but I shall repeat it if you didn't quite comprehend what I said. 'When I was young, I used to wear long socks to hide my skinny legs!'

I know. What was I thinking? I didn't realise, at the time, that I was only accentuating the very thing I was hoping to hide from all my peers. I didn't realise that I was only drawing attention to myself because all the other girls at school wore short socks. The very last thing I wanted to do was draw attention to myself.

But then again, it may have been that nobody took a scrap of notice of what I was wearing. In fact, it may well be that nobody even noticed I had skinny legs in the first place. It's strange how the mind can conjure up all sorts of imaginings, perceiving things to be a certain way. Then you find out sometime later that what one thought was a reality was actually just a figment of one's imagination. Nonetheless, these perceptions were very real to me and impacted the way I felt about myself.

This strange behaviour would indicate to you, I'm sure, that I was very self-conscious. I tended to have very low self-esteem in my younger days. I had quite an inferiority complex that caused me to feel intimidated in the presence of most of my peers. I cannot attribute this to my upbringing, as I grew up in a very positive, loving and stable environment.

It was so geographically stable, in fact, that my parents lived on the same street in Taree for the most part of their lives. Mum grew up at one end of Commerce Street, which adjoined Wingham Road. Dad was raised on Wingham Road, about three kilometres from Mum's place. When they married, they bought a property on ... you guessed it! ... Wingham Road, fair smack in the middle of where they each grew up. They lived there for the next fifty-six years. This was my family home, which is right next door to where my husband and I are now living. My nephew and his family recently became my neighbours, having purchased my parent's place. Mum and Dad had moved to a retirement village just up the road a kilometre or so. My other neighbour is my sister Janine and her husband, David. They bought the house next door on the other side of us. By the way, Janine and David originally owned the home we now live in. They also own the house on the other side of my nephew, who happens to be their son who, as I said, now lives in the place where my parents lived for fifty-six years. Phew ...! Did you get all that?

How is that for stability? I'm sure some would be more inclined to call it stupidity. I have to say, I descended into a fit of giggles just writing it down. You are probably scratching your head, thinking, 'Is this for real?' Yes, I was raised in a very secure and loving environment, both physically and emotionally. Unfortunately, this did not prevent me from feeling very insecure in my own skin.

I might point out that Janine and I have lived in various other places since we initially moved out of home, having married our respective husbands. However, we seem to keep coming back to good old Wingham Road. Very unadventurous, I know!

Apparently, I had a bit of a rough start in life. Immediately after being born in the local hospital in Taree, I was rushed by ambulance to a hospital in Newcastle 170 kilometres away. I was a very sick little baby due to an issue with my blood. Mum and Dad had different blood types that were incompatible, resulting in me needing an emergency blood transfusion. I do not remember any of this, obviously, but thankfully the Lord had His hand on me, and I lived to tell the story.

When I was ten years old, Mum gave birth to a little boy named Daniel. Sadly, he was stillborn due to having the same blood disorder as me. He was swept off immediately to live out his life in heaven. This was the first event I recall that had a significant impact on our family. My parents were devastated by their loss, as were me and Janine. We had been very excited at the prospect of having a new little brother or sister, but sadly it wasn't to be.

Janine is twenty-two months older than me, so we are very close both in age and as sisters. I am grateful to have had a very close network of family surrounding me. I have many wonderful childhood memories of Janine and me playing with cousins. We would play with dolls, make mud pies under the house, ride our bikes, play hockey, have sleepovers, pretend to be witches and fairies, secretaries, and shopkeepers. Not to mention the concerts we used to put together to perform for our parents on sleepover nights. We would use anything we could put our hands on to use as musical instruments and, of course, we all loved singing.

My parents were very gifted musically, both having been raised in musical families. When Janine and I were very young, Mum taught us to sing duets together. Janine would sing the melody line of the tune, and Mum taught me to harmonise by singing the alto part. As a young child, the word 'alto' was one I had not heard before. It was a time in my life when my vocabulary was broadening ever so slightly. I was also learning about Roman numerals at school, 'Roman' was another new word. Unfortunately, in my childish innocence and lack of academic giftedness, I managed to get these two words mixed up on one occasion. I remember excitedly telling our singing teacher, Miss Abbot, that Janine and I were singing duets together. I proclaimed to her ever so proudly, 'Janine sings the melody part, and I sing *Roman.*' Oh, dear! How embarrassing! As you can imagine, our singing teacher was quite amused.

I have to say that my vocabulary, or lack thereof, has caused me to stumble on more than one occasion. I remember one day, I was having a discussion with some family members on this very subject. I managed to confirm my seemingly limited intellect by saying ... 'I don't have a very broad ... (There was a pregnant pause as I tried to think of the appropriate word.) What is that word?' I asked. Then with a bit of prompting, it finally came to me, 'Oh yes ... *vocabulary.*' And I am writing a book? Go figure!

When we were young teenagers, Janine and I, along with four of our cousins formed a singing group. We would sing at various church functions, including travelling to Sydney one year to sing at a large combined youth gathering in the Sydney Town Hall. On another occasion, we were privileged to have the opportunity to be the support act for a Christian singing group called 'Family' who were touring Australia. We sang in the local Civic Theatre. It was quite an honour for us girls at the time.

I have to say, attending school was something I would have quite happily opted out of had I had the choice. This was primarily due to my lack of self-confidence; this continuous lack of belief in my own self-worth extended into my teenage years. I left school and commenced work at the age of fifteen. I always wanted to be a hairdresser, having never really considered that there may actually be other options. I was fortunate enough to gain an apprenticeship resulting in me leaving school halfway through Year Ten, not having acquired my School Certificate or my Higher School Certificate.

My low perception of self only escalated at this time, mainly because my boss used to call me 'pretzel legs' and 'box head.' Yep. That confirmed it for me. I was definitely a misfit. My boss and the other senior hairdressers I worked with were very much into partying, drinking alcohol, smoking cigarettes and other forms of stimulants. On the other hand, I was not only very shy and conservative with a major inferiority complex, but I was also a born-again Christian. Yep. I was definitely right out of my comfort zone; a square peg in a round hole so to speak. (As a side note, all three of my senior hairdressers, including my boss, later became Christians. I am still, to this day, blown away by this. God is so good!)

I'm afraid I may have painted a rather gloomy picture as far as certain aspects of my life are concerned. Please be assured that, for the most part, I have not been totally miserable. It has been quite the opposite, in fact, despite my lack of self-confidence. I feel so blessed to have had such beautiful Christian parents, both having a very quiet and gentle nature. I have a wonderful sister who would always look out for me. I have been fortunate to be blessed with a great bunch of good friends and family, all of whom have contributed to my life in very positive ways.

Though my apprenticeship years didn't seem to be a very positive experience for me at the time, I nonetheless received some excellent training. I acquired a trade that has stood me in good stead. Still, I have often wondered what other path I may have travelled, had I been free enough within myself to look beyond the box and consider other possible careers. That said, all I ever really wanted to do was get married, settle down and have children.

When I was fifteen, not long after leaving school and commencing work, I officially met and started going out with my first boyfriend and future husband, Andrew. I say 'officially met' because I had seen him around town before this. He grew up in Bulahdelah, a small town about 70 kilometres south of Taree. The first time I saw him was at a church youth camp. He was 'going with' another girl at the time.

It's strange how certain things stick in your mind for no fathomable reason. I recall various occasions when I would see Andrew around town, walking up the main street hand in hand with his girlfriend or driving his car past our school. I would be sitting outside having lunch with my girlfriends. I honestly don't recall being particularly attracted to him at that time. Whenever I would see him, it was more a case of me thinking, 'there goes that Andrew guy from camp.' It's strange, though, how he kept popping up, so to speak, and how these random encounters were stored in my memory bank.

When he eventually broke up with his girlfriend, he started coming along to our church with his flatmate. He was working in Taree as a builder at the time, having completed his apprenticeship. He quickly became renowned for flirting with all the girls in our youth group, me excluded, at least at first. I eventually overcame my shyness, and one night, much to my surprise, I reciprocated his advances toward me. He ended up moving back home to Bulahdelah not long after this, although he became a frequent visitor at weekends. Initially, this was a concern to my parents because I was only fifteen, and he was twenty. Nonetheless, our relationship developed and we were married four and a half years later when I was just twenty years of age. My goodness, to be married at twenty seems so young now.

As I said previously, all I ever really wanted in life was to get married and have children. So far so good, it would seem. I was happily married to my one and only serious love. Then along came the second major event that had a massive impact on my life. Just one phone call and my dreams were shattered!

CHAPTER 4

Not Flesh of My Flesh

When I was about nine or ten years old, possibly younger, I received a beautiful baby doll for Christmas, as did one of my cousins. We would spend many hours playing with our dolls and dreaming of the time when we would grow up and get married and have a real baby of our own to love and care for.

Well, the growing up and getting married bit went according to plan. But my life would take a different path than what I initially hoped and imagined when it came to having children. Not long after Andrew and I were married, we decided we wanted to start a family. After a couple of years of trying to conceive without success, we sought the opinion of a doctor who recommended we undergo some tests.

When the test results came back, it wasn't good news. Apparently, due to past trauma there were not enough 'little critters' being produced for fertilisation to take place. The likelihood of conception was one chance in one million.

I still remember that sinking feeling when the doctor gave me the news. As you can probably imagine, I was pretty devastated. It was late one afternoon when the doctor phoned me at work with the results of the tests. I was alone at the time. Andrew had gone to Bulahdelah to play tennis in the local competition that evening. He did, however, forfeit the tennis and drove the hour-long trip home once I managed to contact him with the bad news.

For several months I grieved for a child that would never be born. I couldn't understand why this had to happen to us. I admit to questioning God's purpose in it and feeling quite angry with Him as if He were at fault in allowing this to happen. Despite my anger and feelings of grief and devastation, I still maintained my faith in Him.

As the weeks and months passed, Andrew and I had trouble coming to terms with the reality that we would never have a family of our own. We could not imagine going through life without having children. Before too long, we began to consider the idea of adoption. In the hope of obtaining information on the process and requirements of adoption, we went to see a social worker at the local Department of Youth and Community Services to discuss our options. This proved to be a very discouraging visit. We were told it would be a ten to twelve-year wait to adopt a child from Australia and that overseas adoption was a very challenging and costly process. The social worker was so negative about the idea of overseas adoption that he convinced us it was not worth pursuing. Looking back now, I have my suspicions that he just did not want to be bothered with the whole process.

So, feeling somewhat discouraged and dejected, we decided to put our names down on the long list of people waiting to adopt a child from Australia. A few months later, we heard that my cousin had recently adopted a little girl from Korea. We paid her a visit in the hope of gaining a better understanding of the overseas adoption process. We came away feeling encouraged, deciding we would like to go down this path after all, despite the apparent challenges.

Consequently, the long process of having to cope with miles of red tape and bureaucracy began, which tends to be the case when dealing with Government departments.

In March of 1985, we attended a seminar in Sydney on overseas adoption. One week later, we sent our application forms to the Department of Youth and Community Services to adopt a little girl from Sri Lanka.

In order to adopt a child from overseas, we were required to be assessed and approved as suitable parents by the Australian and Sri Lankan Governments. This would prove to be a very long and frustrating process. We endured several lengthy interviews by a social worker who delved into every detail of our personal lives. Sixteen months later, we finally received our approval letter.

The adoption process continued at this point through an organisation called International Children's Aid. They knew contacts in Sri Lanka who organised our accommodation and travel arrangements and, most importantly, the actual allocation of a child. One of the requirements of the adoption laws in Sri Lanka was that we were to be classed as residents of the country. This meant we were required to stay in Sri Lanka for three weeks once we were allocated a child.

Finally, nineteen months after our application we received notification that we would fly out to Sri Lanka on the 31st of October, 1986. I cannot begin to describe our excitement, knowing we would finally have a baby girl to call our own.

We flew to Sri Lanka with three other couples who were also adopting a baby, one of the couples being from Tinonee, a small town on the outskirts of Taree. We arrived in Sri Lanka at midnight, stepping out onto the tarmac to confront a wall of humid heat. We then endured a one-hour long drive by minibus with a local driver, to the guesthouse where we were to stay in Columbo. Along the way, we were confronted and stopped by soldiers with rifles in hand. They peered in the windows to check who was on board the bus. This was due to the civil war that was happening in the country at the time. A little further down the road, we were pulled over by the police, this time for speeding. These random interruptions were a bit disconcerting and the beginning of a very long three weeks for me. When away from home, I had a tendency to feel homesick at the best of times without having to deal with culture shock as well.

The next day we were up and out of bed early because this was the day we were to meet our babies and their birth mothers. I cannot begin to explain the depth of emotion I was feeling. It was all so very exciting yet quite surreal, not to mention scary, to think we were finally going to meet our little girl.

We arrived at the solicitor's office where the meeting was to take place. Having been ushered into a large sitting room, the moment we had been anticipating for so long finally arrived. Each couple was allocated a child.

Nimali was three weeks old and a tiny little thing at just 2.5 kilos. She had a beautiful tiny little face and long thin limbs that reminded me somewhat of a praying mantis. She was dressed in a little cotton top with a piece of rag for a nappy. She was lying on a very old and threadbare towel that was shredding and fraying around the edges.

It took a while to register in our minds that this little bundle was going to be our little girl. Unfortunately, we didn't get to keep her at this point in time. After signing some papers and spending a little time with her, we reluctantly handed Nimali back to her birthmother, whose name was Karenawathie. She would be required to look after her precious child for another two weeks. How she could do this, knowing the time would come to permanently give her up, is beyond my ability to comprehend or understand.

While all the adoption legalities were being processed, we took the opportunity to do some sightseeing in Sri Lanka. Before this, the mothers and babies of each adoptive couple came to our guesthouse for a visit. The plan was for us to spend some time with them, taking the opportunity to ask any questions we may have and so forth. Then we were to take the babies to the doctor for a check-up. When the minibus arrived, we discovered they had brought the wrong mother with the wrong baby for us. There was some confusion as they tried to convince us this was our baby, but we knew it wasn't Nimali. Eventually, they agreed to go and find her. We were left feeling somewhat concerned, wondering whether Karenawathie had changed her mind. Thankfully, they returned forty minutes later, much to our relief, with Nimali and her mum. Unfortunately, the delay meant we missed out on spending time with them because the babies were due to be taken to the doctor.

When the doctor examined Nimali, he was somewhat concerned that she was so small. He concluded that she must have been born prematurely. Much to our relief, yet again, he gave the go-ahead for the adoption to proceed.

The day finally arrived when we were required to go to court. Karenawathie, Andrew and I stood before the judge to answer several questions and sign some documents. Karenawathie then placed Nimali in my arms and left the room very quickly. The whole experience was quite surreal, and my heart was flooded with a mixture of emotions. I was overjoyed to finally have this beautiful little baby in my arms for keeps. Yet, I was feeling immensely sad for her mother. She had carried this precious little girl for nine months and cared for her as best she could to this point, only to have to give her up for adoption, her circumstances being such that she had neither the means nor the support to continue to care for her. I cannot imagine how difficult this must have been for her.

Our last week in Sri Lanka was spent getting used to having a new little baby to care for. We spent most of the time indoors at the guesthouse, as we were advised against venturing out with the babies for fear of offending the locals. However, we made another trip to the doctor because Nimali had acquired a nasty cough for which the doctor prescribed some medicine. The medication didn't seem to help, and Nimali was still quite ill when it came time to travel home to Australia.

The day we flew out was one of the most exciting days I have experienced and probably the longest I have ever had to endure. This was exacerbated by the fact that we had to contend with Nimali's projectile vomiting due to her illness. Having been inconvenienced with a ten-and-a-half-hour delay at the airport before flying out, our 'day' amounted to 36 hours without sleep. This included a visit to the doctor as soon as we arrived back in Australia so that the babies could be checked over before taking them home. After examining Nimali, the doctor diagnosed her with having a touch of pneumonia. He prescribed some antibiotics, and within a few weeks of our being home, Nimali was a thriving, healthy and absolutely gorgeous little girl.

◇◇◇◇◇◇◇◇

When Nimali was twelve months old, we decided to apply again for a second child, this time for a little boy from India. Without going into all the details, the process of adopting a child from India would turn out to be even more time-consuming and frustrating than the first time around. From the time of application to when our little boy finally arrived in Australia, four and a half years passed by.

About twenty months after applying, we received word that an expectant mother in India was due to give birth '*at any time*', and that he would be ours if she had a little boy. So here we were getting all excited, thinking that we may well be allocated a little baby boy in a week or two. *Six months later,* the mother finally gave birth, and yes, it was a little boy. One month later, we received an allocation letter with our first photo of Christopher. We were obviously very excited. Little did we know at the time though, that another two years and four months would pass by before we would get to hold him in our arms!

Chris spent this whole time in an orphanage in India. Of course, we were very frustrated by this, knowing that the older he became, the harder it would be for him to settle into a new family in a strange country. As we feared, when Chris came to Australia, he was old enough to know he had been taken from everything and everyone he knew and loved in India, yet not old enough to understand what was actually happening or why. It would prove to be a big adjustment for the poor little guy.

Chris and two other children from the orphanage were escorted to Australia by two social workers from India. We travelled to Sydney, where we met them at the airport. We were so excited to be finally meeting our little boy after four and a half years of waiting, waiting and more waiting. On their arrival, Chris was fast asleep in the arms of one of the social workers. In her wisdom, no doubt knowing I would be eager to hold my new little son, she immediately placed him into my arms, which proved to be a wrong move. As soon as he woke and saw my strange 'white' face (as opposed to the 'dark' faces he was used to), he immediately took fright. He began to scream and preferred to have nothing to do with me for the next few days. Every time he looked at me, he cried. I'm sure you can imagine how upsetting this was for me, as selfish as this sounds. Having waited for him for so long, only to have him totally reject me the very minute he laid eyes on me. Thankfully, Andrew managed to win him over reasonably quickly. Chris found a degree of solace in his distress, clinging to Andrew like a little koala for the first few days. He too, was a gorgeous little boy, being pretty small for his age.

A few days later, having arrived back home in Taree, Chris would still have nothing to do with me when my sister Janine came to visit. She decided this lack of bonding between a mother and her son had gone on long enough. She detached Chris' firm grip on Andrew, plopped him into my arms and sent us outside to do some serious mother and son bonding. I spent a while wandering around the yard quietly speaking to him, although he would not have understood a word I was saying. It was a special time, though, and the only time he actually spoke a few words in his own mother tongue. I only wish I had had something on hand to record those few precious words, the last he would speak in his native language.

So, thanks to Janine and her seemingly abrupt actions, things began to improve, although not before Chris spent the next three nights in hospital suffering from very severe vomiting and diarrhoea. It was a Sunday night, and before he took ill, I had decided to go to church. We didn't have mobile phones in those days, but Andrew was able to get word to me via my Dad, to say that he was at the hospital with Chris. Conveniently, the hospital was just across the road from the church. I high-tailed it over the road to find Chris lying limp as a rag doll on the hospital bed. He was a very, very sick little boy. After all that we had been through, we were very much afraid we would lose him before he had a chance to settle into his new home and family. Much to our embarrassment, it turned out that he was suffering from food poisoning, would you believe?

Thankfully, and I'm sure due to lots of people praying for him, he did manage to recover, having spent a few anxious nights in hospital. Over the next few weeks, it was wonderful to see him develop from a very sad and sick little boy into a very happy and healthy child. He adapted to his new surroundings and settled into his new family.

Our family may be a little out of the ordinary, having different coloured skin and cultural beginnings. Yet, we really are just an average family who experiences the usual issues families have to deal with from time to time. Andrew and I have endeavoured to give our children the same secure upbringing we were both blessed to experience as children, having grown up with Christian parents who taught us the ways of God, instilling into our lives the assurance of a God who loves us dearly. A God who, from the very beginning of time, would set a plan into motion whereby He would redeem His 'lost and orphaned' family back to Himself as His beloved children.

As Christians, it is such a comfort to know that no matter what comes our way in life, the Lord has a purpose in it. He can turn what seems to be a bad situation into something good.

> And we know that in all things God works for the good of those who love him, who have been called according to his purpose (Romans 8:28 NIV).

After the immense disappointment of not having the opportunity to experience the miracle of bearing a child, I can testify to the fact that God can turn a negative situation into a positive one. Nimali and Chris are obviously very valuable in God's eyes, as are all of His created beings. Even before they were born, He knew that they would need a mum and a dad who would love and care for them. He knew that Andrew and I would need two beautiful children to complete our family. Although I feel totally inadequate at times, I am so amazingly blessed and humbled to think that God chose me, of all people, to be their mum.

I can say with all sincerity, that I love and adore my children as though I had conceived and carried them myself for nine months in my tummy. Several years ago, I gave Nimali a little plaque with a verse that says it all. It applies to each of my children, of course.

Not flesh of my flesh nor bone of my bone

But still miraculously, my own

Never forget for even a minute

You did not grow under my heart

But in it.

Nimali and Christopher were conceived in my heart long before they were born. They were destined by God to be our children. Through the process of adoption, they now belong to Andrew and me. We are, in every sense of the word, a family. Through adoption, they have taken on a new identity from that which they were born into. They now find their identity and worth as human beings in us, as their parents.

◇◇◇◇◇◇◇◇

God's Word portrays the heart of a loving Heavenly Father who longs to redeem His orphaned children back to Himself, having been estranged from Him at the beginning of time due to sin. His incomprehensible love was such that He gave up His only begotten and beloved Son, Jesus, who became a scapegoat for the sins of many.

> But when the fullness of time had come, God sent forth His Son, born of a woman, born under the law, to redeem those who were under the law, that we might receive the adoption of sons.
>
> And because you are sons, God has sent forth the Spirit of His Son into your hearts, crying out, "Abba Father!" Therefore you are no longer a slave but a son, and if a son, then an heir of God through Christ (Galatians 4:4-7 NKJV).

> Blessed be the God and Father of our Lord Jesus Christ, who has blessed us with every spiritual blessing in the heavenly places in Christ, just as He chose us in Him before the foundation of the world, that we should be holy and without blame before Him in love, having predestined us to adoption as sons by Jesus Christ Himself, according to the good pleasure of His will, to the praise of the glory of His grace, by which He made us accepted in the Beloved (Ephesians 1:3-6 NKJV).

God the Father adopted me into His family as an infant child at the age of nine. It was in God's family that I ultimately discovered my new and true identity. It was in God's family that I eventually knew my God-given value and self-worth.

CHAPTER 5

Enjoying the Milk but I Was Still Hungry

As an infant grows, the drinking of milk alone no longer satisfies. I had been a Christian for many years, yet I had not progressed beyond drinking milk. I was still an infant in Christ, and I was hungry.

'There has to be more,' is what I was thinking. 'There has to be more to being a Christian than what I am currently experiencing!'

I was happily married to my husband Andrew, and we had two beautiful adopted children from overseas. We were very blessed. I was enjoying being a young mum. Generally, life was good, but as far as my life as a Christian was concerned, I was feeling unsettled. *I felt powerless, defeated,* and *spiritually stagnant*, struggling to grow and move forward in my faith.

Just as the Apostle Paul had struggled with his fleshly carnal nature, I battled with mine. Paul says of himself in Romans 7:18–19:

> I know that nothing good lives in me, that is, in my sinful nature. For I have the desire to do what is good, but I cannot

carry it out. For what I do is not the good I want to do; no, the evil I do not want to do – this I keep on doing. (NIV)

Just like Paul, this was the story of my life. As a Christian, I aspired to be more like Jesus, but I seemed to be failing miserably. There were certain things about my behaviour that I was not very proud of. I desperately wanted to change my ways.

About that time, I had a go at writing several songs. The first verse of one of them went like this:

Lord, I seek forgiveness for the sin within my life.

It seems that I have lost control; I want to do what's right.

But time and time again, I find those demons creeping in.

And now my heart is burdened with the shame and guilt of sin.

This verse pretty much describes how I was feeling. Not that I was a really bad person. It may have been something as simple as yelling at the kids when I knew that I should be demonstrating a quiet, gentle spirit, just as I had seen in my mum. I can honestly say that I cannot recall when she ever raised her voice at my sister and me, though there were no doubt many occasions when she would have had good reason to do so. I wanted to be just like her. I had a friend whose mum was a bit of a screamer, and much to my dismay, I was beginning to sound like her, which did not sit well with me at all.

I was at home with my daughter Nimali one day, who was only a toddler at the time. I have no idea what prompted my unseemly behaviour but, for some reason, I was angry, and I yelled at her at the top of my voice. Right at that instant, there was a knock on the front door. I sheepishly went to answer it, and much to my surprise, shock and horror, there standing on the front verandah with a cheeky grin on his face was my uncle who is an ordained 'Reverend' in the Baptist Church. I was so embarrassed. I do not know whether he heard me yelling at the top of my voice, although I suspect he could not have helped but hear me. He was very gracious, nonetheless, and did not say a word. No doubt my profuse blushing was a dead giveaway of how embarrassed I was feeling. After a moment of torturous awkwardness, we both simply chose to grin at each other and pretend it never happened. This incident, and many other similar displays of my fleshly carnal nature, bothered me.

As a born-again Christian, I knew that I had received the Holy Spirit into my heart when I first committed to following Jesus as my Saviour. I learnt from a very young age that the Holy Spirit would help me become a better person. He was my helper and counsellor and guide, and so on. He would enable me to change my inappropriate behaviour, empowering me to become more like Jesus. I knew and believed this to be true, except there was just one problem. I was not experiencing it. I would cry out to the Lord in my frustration, imploring Him to help me change my ways, yet nothing would change. Thus, I began to think that I was missing something. All was not as it should be concerning my walk with the Lord.

Allow me to backtrack a bit. I was very blessed and privileged to have two beautiful Christian parents who raised me in a loving environment with Christian values. They faithfully took my sister Janine and me to the local Baptist Church to attend the service and Sunday school every Sunday. I committed my life to following Jesus as my own personal Saviour in early 1971 when I was nine years old. I clearly remember making this decision in a Sunday school class when a visiting speaker made me realise that I needed to make a choice concerning my belief in Jesus and His teaching. He made me realise that I do not automatically become a Christian just because my parents were Christians. I had to make this decision for myself. I understood the sacrifice Jesus made for me by dying on the Cross to pay the penalty for my sins. After praying a simple prayer, it was at this point in time that I was spiritually born-again, becoming a new babe in Christ. I was adopted into God's family as His redeemed child.

So my walk with the Lord began as an infant child, both physically and spiritually. Through years of being taught at Sunday school and then through my church youth group days and regular church attendance, my faith was nurtured and growing. During my early teenage years, I devoted some time each day to spend with the Lord, reading my Bible and devotionals. I was very keen to grow in my faith. At the age of fifteen, I chose to take the step of being baptised, along with a group of other young people who attended our youth group.

On into my adult years I would go. I do not recall ever experiencing a time where I wavered drastically in my faith, apart from varying degrees of hot and cold occasionally, usually due to life's circumstances. I was comfortable in the Baptist Church. I was satisfied that I was receiving sound Bible-based teaching.

I remember visiting a Pentecostal church with my parents when I was young. They had some friends who were members of the local Assembly of God church. For some reason, we paid them a visit. I remember feeling considerably uncomfortable at the time. Their church service sure was different from what I was used to. There were lots of people waving their arms in the air as they sang, and many were speaking in tongues. As a young child, I did not know what to make of it all. Still, I believe a spark of curiosity was planted in my mind and heart at that time, wondering why I didn't see this in my own church. The only understanding I had concerning the gift of speaking in tongues (which was very little) was that one was best to avoid it unless there was an interpreter present. That was about the extent of it. It was almost as if the subject was taboo. My understanding and views concerning the gift of tongues have changed some since then, but more about that later.

After marrying in 1981, my husband Andrew and I continued to attend the Baptist Church in Taree and then in Sydney, where we lived for about four years. We returned to Taree when our daughter Nimali commenced school because we wanted her to attend the local Christian Community School. It was when Nimali was in Year One that our son Christopher arrived from India. A few years later, I began to feel quite unsettled and stagnant as far as my Christian walk was concerned. I believed that there was so much more to experience as a Christian. This curiosity only increased over the next ten years or so. During this time, I suffered from bouts of depression, causing me to feel even more defeated, both physically and spiritually.

Even though I had been a Christian for many years, I had not progressed beyond being an infant as far as my maturity as a Christian was concerned. I knew Jesus loved me. I knew He had died and rose again to life for me. I was spiritually born-again, having committed to following Jesus as my Saviour. I knew that by the grace of God, my sins were forgiven, and I was destined for heaven when I died. I was nurtured and fed regularly through sound Bible teaching. I desired with all my heart to reflect the character of Jesus and strove with all my might to be more like Him, but ... *I was still failing miserably*! I was still hungry for more of *something*! That gnawing feeling that *something* was missing would not go away! *And then it happened*!

PART II

Hearing God's Voice

CHAPTER 6

Learning to Hear God's Voice

I have sat in churches for many years, soaking up the teaching of God's Word on many varied topics by highly regarded preachers and pastors I greatly respect. Yet, I do not recall having ever heard from the pulpit about hearing God's voice, or more specifically, *how* to hear God's voice. My lack of understanding in this area has rendered my walk with the Lord less than it should have been. My *'dulled hearing'* and inability to decipher God's voice and leading contributed to my spiritually stagnant condition.

It is the hearing of God's voice through the written and spoken word that produces and waters the seed of faith.

> So then faith comes by hearing, and hearing by the word of God (Romans 10:17 NKJV).

It is imperative to my growth and maturity as a Christian that I not only *hear* God's voice, but I must heed every word, obedient to His every command. The consequences of failing to be obedient to God have been evident since the beginning of time when Adam and Eve first fell from grace due to disobedience. God's chosen race, the Israelites, suffered under curses instead of blessings due to their disobedience and failure to do as God commanded. Only as they recognised their failure to heed His voice and repent of their wicked ways did God forgive their sins and acknowledge them again as His people.

When we recognise and obey God's voice, He claims us as His own, as affirmed by Jesus in the following verses:

> My sheep hear My voice, and I know them, and they follow Me. And I give them eternal life, and they shall never perish; neither shall anyone snatch them out of My Father's hand (John 10:27-28 NKJV).

> Then Jesus said to those Jews who believed Him, "If you abide in My word, you are My disciples indeed. And you shall know the truth, and the truth shall make you free" (John 8:31-32 NKJV).

In the natural scheme of things, we can only recognise a person's voice if we know them personally and are associated with them regularly, whether they be a relative, friend or associate. It is impossible to recognise the voice of a stranger.

Sheep recognise the voice of their shepherd, trusting him to lead them beside still waters where they can drink and be refreshed and into green pastures where they can relax and rest under his protection. They know that the shepherd will take care of their every need.

As I get to know my Good Shepherd personally, I learn to hear and recognise His voice. I get to know Him through His Word and begin to trust Him, knowing He loves me and will take care of me. Just as sheep rest under the protection of their shepherd, having an ear tuned to his voice, I hear the gentle whisper of the Holy Spirit as I relax in a place of *spiritual rest*.

> I am the good shepherd; and I know My sheep, and am known by My own. As the Father knows Me, even so I know the Father; and I lay down My life for the sheep. And other sheep I have which are not of this fold; them also I must bring, and they hear My voice; and there will be one flock and one shepherd (John 10:14-16 NKJV).

God does not usually speak with an audible voice, although some can testify to this being their experience. God's voice is a gentle prompting of His

Spirit that deposits a sense of assurance deep in my heart and soul, causing me to know in my very being that God has spoken. God communicates with His children in many ways, including through dreams, visions, impressions and the depositing of thoughts into our minds, sometimes in the form of words of wisdom or knowledge. But usually, it is through His still small voice in the promptings of His Holy Spirit, most often and most importantly through His Word, the Holy Scriptures, as affirmed in 2 Timothy 3:16-17.

> All Scripture is given by inspiration of God, and *is* profitable for doctrine, for reproof, for correction, for instruction in righteousness, that the man of God may be complete, thoroughly equipped for every good work. (NKJV)

The following are a few short stories of when I first began to consciously be open to hearing God's voice. I emphasise that these were very much *'learning'* experiences! Not everybody's journey is the same. God speaks to us in different ways, when and how He so pleases.

I had every desire to grow in my faith, yet I wallowed in a state of spiritual stagnancy for a time. But the more I get to know my Heavenly Husband through His Word, the more confident I am in recognising His voice. I write this not as an expert but as one who has been learning along the way and is aware I still have much to learn. I hope the experiences I share may be of some encouragement to others, even if it is simply in knowing that we all make mistakes along the way.

It was a time in my life when the Lord expanded my view and knowledge of Him, opening my eyes to the enormity of His love and desire to communicate with His children, His Bride. During this time of being open to God's leading through various life experiences, He began to unblock my fleshly mindset, the *dormant mind* that kept me bound and unable to move forward in my walk with Him. I was hungry for more in my experience as a Christian. I longed to be empowered by the Holy Spirit, to be controlled by Him instead of my fleshly human nature. This hunger was the catalyst that began to grow me into knowing my Heavenly Husband more intimately. I was far from being confident in hearing God's voice, yet the following experiences taught me some valuable lessons along the way.

God speaks to a Hungry and Expectant Heart

I learnt through the following experience that God never 'motivates' us to do His will through negative emotions such as fear and anxiety. I misunderstood my feelings of being compelled to 'take action' with that of being convicted by the Holy Spirit. I believed I was in God's will. Compulsions are motivated by the flesh. Convictions are motivated by the Holy Spirit when based on the truths of God's Word. Also, 'thoughts' do not necessarily come from God. As Christians, the Holy Spirit dwells in our hearts, but this does not guarantee that our will aligns with God's will.

It seemed that I was driven by a force that left me powerless to give in to reason. I later asked myself . . . 'Was I driven by God through the leading of His Holy Spirit? Or was I driven by the king of deception, Satan, him causing me to *believe* that I was in God's will? Or were my actions all simply part of God's plan, ultimately causing me to learn, discern and grow in my walk with Him?'

It was about July 2009. Our daughter Nimali and her boyfriend Ben (not his real name) had been going together for three years. Things were going along fine when, suddenly their relationship fell apart.

It was the beginning of a journey that took me on a roller-coaster ride of emotions. It was also a time of spiritual awakening and growth that I had not previously known in my many years of being a Christian.

Not long before this turn of events, I became interested in Derek Prince's teachings. Since the age of fifteen, I have spent time daily reading God's Word, or at least a daily devotional, which kept me on a steady walk with the Lord. In recent times, however, I had a real hunger to grow in my faith, sensing there was so much more to being a Christian than what I was experiencing. As I listened to the teachings of Derek Prince, I began to believe that he may have the answers I had been searching for. I also became more aware of the rampant spiritual warfare in the heavenly realms and here on earth.

Getting back to Nimali and Ben, I was convinced that Satan played a major role in tearing apart their relationship, and I was determined to fight on their behalf. I believed then that it was God's will that Nimali and Ben be together. Time would prove otherwise, but before this became evident, I took it upon myself to 'fix' their relationship. I wrote quite a few letters to Ben in the hope of helping him understand things from Nimali's perspective. In doing so, I endeavoured to be sensitive, trying to imagine and understand how he was feeling. I became involved to a degree that amounted to obsessive interference. My fear and anxiety for Nimali's wellbeing caused me to act out of compulsion, yet for a number of reasons, I sincerely believed that the Holy Spirit was leading me.

To cut a very long story short, as the conflict escalated between Nimali and Ben, I began to question whether it *was* God's will that they be together, or was it simply what I wanted at the time. Trying to justify my feelings and my actions, I reasoned to myself (quite unreasonably). *'If I have the Holy Spirit living within me, then wouldn't it be reasonable to assume that my 'thoughts' must be in line with God's 'thoughts?' That my will is in line with God's will?'*

For years, I had known in my heart that, as a Christian, my body is a temple of the Holy Spirit, as God's Word tells us in 1 Corinthians 6:19. Yet, in my fragile state, I felt that I needed proof that this was, in fact, the case. In desperation, I prayed one night that God might prove to me that His Holy Spirit was dwelling within me. I asked Him to grant to me the gift of speaking in tongues. I also prayed that He would make His will clear to me concerning Nimali and Ben's future. I cried out desperately to the Lord that night, seeking answers. I went to bed and waited with an expectant heart to hear from the Lord.

God Speaks in a Dream

Vivid dreams are not necessarily from the Lord. They can be from the devil or our flesh. If the theme or message aligns with our heart, the dream is from our flesh. If the theme or message causes fear or anxiety, it is from the devil. If the theme or message takes us by surprise, is totally 'new' to us, and causes us to seek God for further information or confirmation, then it probably is from the Lord.

I woke in the early hours of the morning with a start, having had a dream. It went like this:

I was at a women's camp. I found myself in a big hall with other women around. Two strawberry pies were sitting on the table. I picked them up and stood for what seemed like an eternity, holding possessively onto these pies. They were mine. I had claimed them for myself. Then, for some reason, I very briefly put them back on the table to do something. Next thing, when I turned around to pick them up again, they were gone. Two other ladies had claimed them as their own. My cheeks blew-up like enormous balloons as I desperately wanted to defend my right to those pies. But I couldn't say a word because I had a button firmly attached to my lips. As frustrated as I felt because I had lost my pies, I had to walk away and let them go. I had to come to terms with the fact that the pies were no longer in my possession.

I woke from this dream knowing it was from the Lord, but in the first instance, I misinterpreted its meaning. It was many months after Nimali and Ben broke up before I would finally understand and accept the correct interpretation of this dream. I knew in my heart what the Lord would have me do.

The two pies I was zealously protecting were Nimali and Ben. I was holding on to them with all my might, unprepared to let them go. I was not about to give them up without a fight. In the end, this is what the Lord would have me do. I had been defending Nimali to Ben and Ben to Nimali for many months. The Lord was very clearly telling me that it was time to put them back on the table. I needed to 'put the button on my lips' and stop my defensive behaviour. It was time to leave them in the Lord's hands. As the Lord would have it, just as two other people took up the two pies in my dream, so too, were Nimali and Ben. They both moved on to new relationships with other people.

God Speaks in a Vision

As I mentioned before – If a dream or vision takes us by surprise and is totally 'new' to us, causing us to seek further information or confirmation, it is most likely of the Lord. I am certain this vision I experienced was from the Lord. It took me by surprise. Here's what happened.

That same night, after the dream, God spoke to me again through a vision. I had drifted into a semi-conscious state when something flashed before my eyes so quickly that I felt as though I almost missed it. I saw a computer screen. In the middle of the screen, on an 'activator button' or icon, the following words were written in capital letters:

PREPARATION FOR DESTINATION

Having woken with a start, I briefly pondered what I saw in my vision. In my semi-conscious state, I continued to envisage the computer screen and mentally 'clicked' on the activator button on which was written 'preparation for destination'. In my mind, I found myself entering God's throne room. Just as a computer is full of knowledge, I felt like I was entering into God's 'knowledge', into the realm of God's omniscience. It was there that I lay down at His feet and *rested*, knowing that *He knew* what the future held and that *He was in control*.

Both the dream and the vision were genuine to me, yet, in both instances, I initially misinterpreted their meaning. I believed the Lord would have me understand through this vision that He was preparing Nimali and Ben for the future. I would realise some time later that its message was more applicable to *me* than to Nimali and Ben.

God Speaks in a Still Small Voice

The still small voice often referred to is the Holy Spirit speaking. His voice is not loud but more like a whisper in our hearts. If we truly seek to hear His voice, we must be still, focus, and listen with our heart, resting in His presence. It is interesting to note that the words

> *'ear', 'hear' and 'heart' are very closely connected. We hear with our ears, and we hear with our heart, the latter most especially when it comes to hearing God's voice.*

Getting back to when I found myself resting in the presence of the Lord, laying at His feet and relaxing in the knowledge that all was well and He was in control. In the quietness, He spoke to me again, this time in His still, small voice. At this moment, the Lord addressed my prayer request that He grant me the gift of speaking in tongues. In the quietness, He spoke in a whisper. He informed me gently that the gift of speaking in tongues is not the only indication or evidence of God's presence within. He told me that the *gift of prophecy* also indicates His indwelling Spirit.

Then, I was considerably ignorant concerning the gift of prophecy; this was a confirmation for me that the Lord had spoken. As I pondered on all that had occurred in the early hours of that morning, I decided I would seek out what God had to say in His Word concerning this gift. I later went to my Bible and found 1 Corinthians 14:1-5:

> Pursue love, and desire spiritual *gifts*, but especially that you may prophesy. For he who speaks in a tongue does not speak to men but to God, for no one understands *him*; however, in

the spirit he speaks mysteries. But he who prophesies speaks edification and exhortation and comfort to men. He who speaks in a tongue edifies himself, but he who prophesies edifies the church. I wish you all spoke with tongues, but even more that you prophesied; for he who prophesies is greater than he who speaks with tongues, unless indeed he interprets, that the church may receive edification. (NKJV)

I had little awareness or understanding of the gift of prophecy, except in the context of the Old Testament Prophets, who received clear and unmistakable revelations from God. I may need to clarify here. The gift of prophecy does not necessarily qualify one to be considered a Prophet, as if being equal to the spiritual stature of the Old Testament Prophets. However, many such anointed Prophets and Prophetesses hold this office, even today.

The Apostle Paul spoke to the Corinthians concerning the gift of prophecy and how it applies to the Church:

> For you can all prophesy one by one, that all may learn and all may be encouraged (1Corinthians 14:31 NKJV).

Paul states here that *'all* can prophesy'. The gift of prophecy is available to all who press into God's Word, fully submitted to doing His will and sensitive to the promptings of the Holy Spirit, to His still small voice. God gives this gift for the purpose of instruction and encouragement and the building up of the saints.

When walking closely with the Lord and open to His leading in any given situation, we can expect Him to communicate with us in whatever way He sees fit. I was beginning to realise that God is willing to speak with me whilst I have ears to hear and a heart that yearns to know and do His will. I had gone to bed that night *expecting* to hear from the Lord. I feel humbled and privileged that He would choose to make His will known to me through a dream, a vision and His still small voice.

> Then He said, "Hear now My words: "If there is a prophet among you, I, the LORD, make Myself known to him in a **vision**; I speak to him in a **dream** (Numbers 12:6 NKJV). [Emphasis mine].

I might just say that I do not presume to have the gift of prophecy, nor to be a prophet. But the Lord gave me a little taste of what is available to me if I truly desire to hear His voice and seek more in my relationship with Him. My curiosity heightened from this experience, so I decided to do some more research. I discovered a book called *You May All Prophesy* written by Steve Thomson. I was blown away by the heading of chapter five in the book:

PREPARATION FOR INTERPRETATION

This heading took me quite by surprise because it was similar both in word and format to the vision I had seen, being PREPARATION FOR DESTINATION. Coming across this heading caused a quickening in my spirit, leaving me with a sense that the Lord was trying to tell me something. I wondered whether I mistook the word 'interpretation' for 'destination' in the vision I saw that night. It had flashed in front of me so quickly that I felt as though I almost missed it. Whatever the case, both were very applicable at the time and a confirmation for me that the Lord had spoken. He was *preparing* me for the correct interpretation of the dream and the vision. He was also preparing me, through these experiences, for whatever the future holds, according to His will and *destiny* for my life.

God Speaks Through a Word of Knowledge

Sometimes God reveals things to come in the future through words of knowledge, inner awareness or supernatural knowledge of something outside of our natural realm of knowledge. I mentioned previously not every 'thought' we have is necessarily in line with God's will. In the following instance, I believe the 'thoughts' that came to me were from God, revealing His will concerning Nimali's future.

It was the very same morning that Nimali and Ben first broke up. Nimali had phoned me in the early morning hours, in tears and completely devastated. I jumped out of bed and high-tailed it to Newcastle, two hours away, to be with her. I crawled into her bed and gave her a big cuddle. As I lay there with her, quietly praying to myself that all would be well, I distinctly remember a *'thought'* going through my mind that *twelve months* would pass before the situation would be resolved. I also *'thought'* that the *Lord would provide someone else for her* if things didn't work out with Nimali and Ben. A *pastor's son* had entered my mind. I had a fleeting sense or feeling that this person would come from *the southern side of Newcastle!*

I didn't think much of it at that moment, putting such thoughts to the back of my mind. Yet, everything I 'thought' back then is exactly what came to fruition. It was twelve months from when Nimali and Ben first broke up to when things resolved. Matthew came onto the scene a few months later. He lived on the southern side of Newcastle, his dad being a pastor at the local Baptist Church.

It would seem that the Lord gave me a *word of knowledge* concerning His plans for Nimali right back at the beginning of her problems with Ben. I believe the Lord assured me that all would be well with Nimali. Had I realised this then, I would have saved us a whole lot of grief. On the other hand, I would not have had the opportunity to learn valuable lessons, causing me to mature and grow in my walk with the Lord. I am learning to have a listening ear, to be more *in tune with* and *yielded to* His Holy Spirit so that I can hear and be sensitive to His voice and leading more confidently.

I am so grateful for God's wonderful provision for Nimali in her husband, Matthew. God knew that they were destined for each other, and I couldn't be happier. They met through mutual friends who had decided a couple of years beforehand to introduce them if circumstances prevailed. Their friends believed they would make a good couple because they both attended church. I have no doubt this was all part of God's provision for Nimali.

In His foreknowledge, God *saw* Nimali's need well before all this happened and made perfect *provision* for her in advance. Twelve months before they met, the Lord tried to tell me of His plans for Nimali and Matthew through a *word of knowledge*, but unfortunately, I didn't recognise His voice at the time.

God Speaks Through His Word

> *God does not condone using individual scripture verses to 'support' our own will and desires or to justify pursuing our selfish ambitions, particularly if in doing so we break a General Principle or Law of God. Yet, if we are genuinely seeking the Lord's will in a matter, He can quicken scripture verses to us, bringing them to our mind to lead and guide us when making important decisions. However, it is very easy to see what we want to see sometimes, and we need to be cautious that our own selfish desires are not misleading us.*

For many years, I have been aware of the benefits of memorising scripture and keeping God's Word in my heart, helping me navigate this life journey. However, as I suffered in my *spiritually stagnant* condition with a *dormant mind* and *complacency* when it came to an in-depth study of God's Word, I could not recite and recall scripture as I ought. Yet, as I grappled with knowing God's will when making important decisions, by His grace, the Holy Spirit would sometimes deposit references of 'unknown' passages of scripture in my mind that were relevant to my situation. They would hint at how I should go, or at least teach me lessons along the way. I knew I needed to be very cautious in this, not assuming too much without further confirmation.

For example –Andrew, and I had the opportunity to purchase the home of one of my uncles. We were not considering buying a property at that time. We had struggled financially and didn't think the bank would lend us the money to do so. Nonetheless, we decided to ask the Lord what we should do. One morning, as I was praying for God's leading, I came to a passage I was not familiar with in Isaiah 54:2.

> Enlarge the place of your tent, And let them stretch out the curtains of your dwellings; Do not spare; Lengthen your cords, and strengthen your stakes. (NKJV)

You may well be able to imagine my awe and amazement as I contemplated what this verse was saying. If this was from the Lord, as I believed it was, it seemed to indicate that perhaps He would have us consider the possibility of expanding our assets. I decided to look at this passage in a different version of the Bible. As I was rummaging through my drawer, I came across a little book called *The Prayer of Jabez* by Bruce Wilkinson. It is about a righteous man in the Old Testament. He prayed a simple prayer to the Lord according to 1 Chronicles 4:10.

And Jabez called on the God of Israel saying, "Oh, that You would bless me indeed, and **enlarge my territory**, that Your hand would be with me, and that You would keep me from evil, that I may not cause pain!" So God granted him what he requested. (NKJV) [Emphasis mine].

My coming across this little book was no accident, I believe. I had before me two verses of scripture. One spoke of enlarging one's tent and the other of enlarging one's territory. In light of these verses, I felt that we should at least consider purchasing my uncle's house. Andrew and I believed the Lord would close the door if this were not, in fact, His will.

To begin with, and much to our excitement, doors began to open, and it looked as though we could purchase the property after all, despite our financial situation. Yet, as it turned out, after much deliberating with banks and accountants etc., and for various other reasons, that particular door eventually closed. Although, I am not sure whether the Lord closed the door or I did, quite frankly.

Though we may have every desire to hear God's voice and be obedient to His leading, I am very much aware that I can still get it wrong. Nonetheless, several years later, having sold our home in Taree and having moved to Bulahdelah, we did eventually purchase a 'fixer-upper' investment property right next door, which proved to be God's provision of work for Andrew (and myself) during 'pandemic' lockdowns. A lesson learnt in this experience was that God's timing is quite often very different to mine. He is also a God of second chances when we don't get things right in the first instance. In His foreknowledge, He knew our needs further down the track.

◇◇◇◇◇◇◇◇

On another occasion, Andrew and I received several phone calls from a rather pushy salesperson trying to convince us to buy an expensive computer program that would assist in the purchasing of shares in the stock market. Due to our somewhat dire financial situation, we weren't in a position to purchase said program, however, this man was very persuasive. (Now that's an understatement. Downright manipulative is probably a better description). The more we insisted that we could not afford the program, the more he tried to convince us that we couldn't afford *not* to buy it.

Again, I sought the Lord's leading, praying that He would show me whether we should *invest* in the *share* market. I was hoping for a verse of scripture to give me a clear lead as to the Lord's will on this matter. The thought went through my mind that it would be unlikely that the word 'shares' would be found in the Bible. Certainly not in the context of stock market shares, and I wondered how the Lord might lead me in this. Just then, 'Micah 4' came to mind. I searched for this passage in my Bible, hoping it was a prompting of the Holy Spirit. When I found it, I was shocked. A heading at the top of the page read *'Swords into Plowshares'* [Emphasis mine].

Of course, the word 'plowshares' has nothing to do with trading shares in the stock market. Nonetheless, I could not help but wonder whether the Lord had directed me to this passage for a purpose. Was this a sign indicating that we should go down this path of investing in shares? I was far from convinced, yet I resolved to be open-minded and continue to wait on the Lord for direction.

Cutting yet another long and rather excruciating story short, after many phone calls from this man, I became confused as to what I should do due to his incessant determination to make a sale. He even challenged my integrity in the process. I have never experienced such an onslaught of determined and manipulative pressure and temptation in all my life.

You may be asking yourself, 'Why didn't she just hang up the phone for crying out loud?' I certainly had considered this, but I was so caught up in the temptation, bound by indecision and confusion. In the back of my mind was the word 'plow**shares**'. I believed the Lord had shown me this for a reason, but at this point, I wasn't sure why.

After hanging up the phone for the umpteenth time, I desperately cried out to the Lord for help. In His still small voice, He immediately directed me to Proverbs 3.

A wonderful sense of peace washed over me as I read the chapter. The following verses particularly spoke into my spirit, giving me more clarity in my thoughts as I read them.

> Trust in the LORD with all your heart, And lean not on your own understanding; In all your ways acknowledge Him, And He shall direct your paths. Do not be wise in your own eyes; Fear the Lord and depart from evil.

> Honor the LORD with your possessions, And with the firstfruits of all your increase; So your barns will be filled with plenty, And your vats will overflow with new wine.

> Happy is the man who finds wisdom, And the man who gains understanding; For her proceeds are better than the profits of silver, And her gain than fine gold. She is more precious than rubies, And all the things you may desire cannot compare to her. Length of days is in her right hand, In her left hand riches

and honor. Her ways are ways of pleasantness, and all her paths are peace.

... Keep sound wisdom and discretion; So they will be life to your soul And grace to your neck. Then you will walk safely in your way, And your foot will not stumble.

Do not envy the oppressor, And choose none of his ways; For the perverse person is an abomination to the Lord, But His secret counsel is with the upright. (NKJV)

Reading this passage released me from the stronghold of confusion Satan had over me that day, helping me gain perspective concerning things of importance in life. The Lord reminded me that sound wisdom is far better than the proceeds of silver and gold. Finding our *security* in material possessions and monetary gain is not the Lord's intent and purpose for His children. That is not to say that He does not desire to bless us with such things, but possessing them should not be our first priority.

Just as in the saga of potentially purchasing my uncle's property, we did not go down this path of investing in shares either, but there was a lesson to be learnt here concerning the importance of *investing*.

The reference in Micah 4 speaks of the Latter-Days when God will fully establish His kingdom on earth. 'Turning swords into plowshares' was a reference symbolising the end of the war against humanity, converting the sword, being a means or weapon of destruction, into a creative tool that would benefit humanity.

I learnt through this process of seeking God's will concerning *investing* that rather than being overly concerned with investing in this world and its material benefits, I firstly and most importantly need to *invest in the kingdom of God,* both financially through tithes and offerings, and especially by investing in my relationship with Jesus. Not discounting the fact that I still need to make wise choices concerning my everyday finances, but I was reminded that my present and future *security* is not found in earthly investments. It is only found in the saving grace of my God, who promises to supply all of my needs.

> "Therefore do not worry, saying, 'What shall we eat?' or 'What shall we drink?' or 'What shall we wear?' For after all these things the Gentiles seek. For your heavenly Father knows that you need all these things. **But seek first the kingdom of God and His righteousness, and all these things shall be added to you.** Therefore do not worry about tomorrow, for tomorrow

will worry about its own things. Sufficient for the day is its own trouble (Matthew 6:31-34 NKJV). [Emphasis mine].

One morning, I was having a little chat with the Lord as I was eating my breakfast. I simply asked Him what He would have me learn from Him that day. As I stilled myself and listened for a response, the words *'create in me a clean heart, oh God, and renew a steadfast spirit within me'* came to mind.

I knew this was a passage of scripture, but I was also aware that it was a song we sang in church occasionally. I sceptically thought that maybe I had heard the song recently, and it came to mind. Having just sought the Lord for direction for my day, however, I thought it wise to consider this to be a word from Him. I had no idea where this passage was in scripture, so I asked the Lord where I might find it. Immediately, Psalm 51 came to mind. I anxiously turned to the passage, and there it was. Psalm 51:10-13.

> Create in me a clean heart, O God, And renew a steadfast spirit within me. Do not cast me away from Your presence, And do not take Your Holy Spirit from me. Restore to me the joy of Your salvation, And uphold me by Your generous Spirit.

> Then I will teach transgressors Your ways, And sinners shall be converted to You. (NKJV)

Once again, I cannot express my excitement and the overwhelming sense of awe that I felt when I turned to this passage, and there were the words I was hoping to see in front of me.

Though these moments may not necessarily be typical of how the Lord speaks to us generally, these experiences drew me closer to my Heavenly Husband, giving me a burning desire and a hunger to know Him more intimately.

The Lord takes great delight in sending us on a big treasure hunt, enticing us to seek out more of His treasures. With each treasure I find and experience of Him, I desire to seek out more. He is a loving Father who longs to give His children good gifts. He longs for me to get to know Him so intimately that I can easily hear and recognise His voice and sense His presence with me every minute of the day, when I lay down to sleep and when I wake in the morning.

The scripture passage the Lord whispered into my spirit that day in Psalm 51 has become a regular prayer of mine. It reminds me of my ongoing need for the steadfast presence of the Holy Spirit within me. His abiding presence causes me to know and experience the joy of my salvation, rendering me useful in His service.

There is more to learn from this passage in Psalm 51. My heart needs to be clean and open to hearing from the Lord. I am not referring here to my physical heart that pumps blood and keeps me alive physically, but that special place deep inside that God designed to harbour His precious Holy Spirit, keeping me alive spiritually. It is in my heart that God places His will and purposes for my life.

It is also where I can harbour unrepented sin and selfish ambitions, causing me to stumble and fall out of God's will. In this case, I must recognise my sin and confess it to my Heavenly Father, knowing that He is faithful and just to forgive my sins and cleanse me from all unrighteousness (1 John 1:9 NKJV).

The content and condition of my heart determines the path I walk and the direction my life will take. As I incline my ear to God's Word and keep it in my heart, being obedient to it, I can trust that God's best intentions for me will be realised.

> My son, give attention to my words; Incline your ear to my sayings. Do not let them depart from your eyes; Keep them in the midst of your heart; For they are life to those who find them, And health to all their flesh. Keep your heart with all

diligence, For out of it spring the issues of life (Proverbs 4:20-23 NKJV).

Over the years, I have grappled with the various symptoms of spiritual stagnation, including *dulled hearing, a dormant mind and complacency*, all of which kept me from hearing God's voice and retaining God's Word in my heart; this was due to a lack of in-depth study and memorising of scripture. Keeping God's Word in my heart is paramount in knowing my Good Shepherd intimately. I long to be constantly immersed in His presence and ever alert to His voice, to be so intimately connected with Him that I am empowered, through His Holy Spirit, to be all that He would have me to be and thereby live out my life in the very centre of His will.

PART III

Spiritual Growth

CHAPTER 7

My Battle with Depression

'Antidepressants! They ought to put them in our drinking water!' This was a snide remark made by one of my cousins because so many of our relatives, including her and myself, have suffered from depression. She thought it would make good sense to have our antidepressant medication on tap, so to speak, for easy access. She was joking, of course. Though I took this in good humour, anyone who has suffered from this debilitating illness will know it is anything but a joking matter. It is quite the opposite, in fact.

I had suffered from a degree of depression on and off over several years, although not to the extent of some of my relatives, who have been considerably debilitated with the illness at times.

Many years ago, I was sitting at my dining room table just gazing out the back window, which overlooks the local golf course. We are very blessed to have a beautiful view of green fairways extending from our fence line, looking down across rolling hills and valleys. At the bottom of the lowest gully is a creek lined with trees and bushes. Beyond the trees, we used to see the local farms that extended for miles across the flats and further to more hills on the distant horizon. The trees have grown considerably taller now, so our view of the farms and distant mountains has been restricted somewhat, but it is still beautiful.

I was sitting there gazing through my window at the beautiful scenery before me, yet I was unable to fully grasp or comprehend the beauty it portrayed. It was a fine day with cloudless blue skies, but hovering just above my head was a big black cloud that seemed to extend from where I was sitting in my dining room, reaching right across to the distant horizon. Of course, there was no such black cloud, although it seemed so very real to me at the time. I recall feeling as though I were totally weighed down under a blanket of darkness. Andrew and I were struggling financially, and I was not particularly enjoying my work, but generally, life was good. I was very blessed in so many ways, but I could not seem to shake this feeling of being downcast and depressed.

I would resort to antidepressant medication occasionally, though this did not sit well with me. It bothered me, being a Christian, that this illness would have such a stronghold on me. I knew that Christ had died and rose again so that I might know the abundance and fullness of life, yet this was not my experience. I understood that depression was an illness brought about by a chemical imbalance in the brain. Nonetheless, it was an illness that I did not want hanging over my life because it was stealing my joy, a joy that I believed should have been mine as a Christian.

Several years later, during the twelve months I spoke of when Nimali and Ben broke up, I was at my lowest point with depression. I was so unwell that I had to take a few days off work at one point. My depression caused me to lose my appetite, resulting in me losing ten kilos in weight. I knew there was medical evidence to support the fact that depression is due to a chemical imbalance in the brain, but I had my suspicions that Satan was at the heart of this debilitating condition. I began to recognise that he was manipulating my life by attacking my mind, gaining a stronghold that was causing me to feel defeated and almost powerless to withstand his ploys to keep me down.

At my lowest point, when I needed antidepressants more than ever, I decided I did not want to fight my depression with the help of medication any longer. I had come to believe that I was under spiritual attack by Satan and his demons, and I was ready to take him on. It was at this point that I chose to take myself off my medication. (Please note, this is my experience, and I am not suggesting that any of my readers take such drastic measures without medical advice.)

And so began my conquest to defeat my adversary the devil, and his army of demons. The Lord had been teaching me through His Word, also through the experiences and teachings of others, just how I could have the victory over this mental illness. Over time, and with ongoing perseverance, I have slowly but surely been released from the stronghold of Satan.

Deliverance through Confession and Praise

My initial and ongoing line of attack to overcome my depression is through the *praise* and *confession* of my mouth of Jesus and His redeeming sacrifice. Through faith in the power of His shed blood poured out on my behalf at Calvary, I am placed in a position of authority over Satan, enabling me to defeat him and his attempts to bring me down. As soon as I find myself sinking into a negative frame of mind, I verbally renounce Satan through the blood of Jesus and lift up my voice to God in praise and worship. In Isaiah 61 we are told that Jesus came to heal the broken-hearted, to proclaim liberty to the captives and the opening of the prison to those who are bound. He came to comfort all who mourn and give them the oil of joy for mourning and *the garment of praise for the spirit of heaviness.*

When I clothe myself in the garment of praise and freely lift up the name of Jesus in worship, the spirit of heaviness that manifests itself in me is defeated. As the precious name of Jesus is lifted high and proclaimed as the name above all names, Satan and his demons cower and flee.

I have become more aware in recent times that the spoken word is powerful. God created the world and brought it into being through His spoken word. When Jesus spent forty days in the wilderness after His baptism, He fended off the attacks of Satan by quoting words of Scripture. When I confess and speak out loud the truths and the promises of God's Word, I am empowered to overcome Satan and his attempts to take control of my mind by filling my thoughts with his lies, causing me to focus on the negatives of life instead of the positives. The more I proclaim the precious name of Jesus in worship and song, the more I experience a new sense of well-being begin to wash over me.

Deliverance through the Armour of God

I am reminded in Ephesians 6:10-17 that I need to put on the whole armour of God to fend off the attacks of the evil one:

> Finally, my brethren, be strong in the Lord and in the power of His might. Put on the whole armour of God, that you may

be able to stand against the wiles of the devil. For we do not wrestle against flesh and blood, but against principalities, against powers, against the rulers of the darkness of this age, against spiritual hosts of wickedness in the heavenly places. Therefore, take up the whole armour of God, that you may be able to withstand in the evil day, and having done all, to stand.

Stand therefore, having girded your waist with truth, having put on the breastplate of righteousness, and having shod your feet with the preparation of the gospel of peace; above all, taking the shield of faith with which you will be able to quench all the fiery darts of the wicked one. And take the **helmet of salvation,** and the **sword of the Spirit, which is the word of God.** (NKJV) [Emphasis mine].

When the Word of God is spoken out boldly, it becomes a double-edged sword that pierces through the darkness that hangs over my life, dispelling the spirit of heaviness that causes me to feel downcast and depressed.

From a medical perspective, depression is a mental illness affecting the soundness of my mind. It is my mind that needs to be protected from Satan's attack. According to Ephesians 6:17, it is the *helmet* of salvation that would stand to be the piece of armour that I need to protect my head, or my mind, as it were.

> But let us who are of the day be **sober**, putting on the breastplate of faith and love, and as a **helmet** the **hope** of salvation (1Thessalonians 5:8 NKJV). [Emphasis mine]

This verse speaks to me of my need to remain sober, to have a clear and sound mind, and always be ready and alert to stand firm against the wiles of the devil. The *hope of my salvation* in Christ protects my mind from falling into the pit of darkness and depression. This *hope* is not a flimsy and fragile form of wishful thinking that lacks a firm foundation on which it is based. It is derived from and grounded in the *faith* I have in Christ, my Saviour, who descended into the very depths of hell and darkness to conquer death and darkness and evil on my behalf, rendering me free to live out my life in the light of His salvation. As a redeemed child of God, I am equipped and empowered to defeat Satan. He does his utmost to have me wallow in deep-seated negative thoughts and overly indulgent self-focus, which basically amounts to self-pity.

With the *hope* of salvation as my helmet, I have every reason to live my life with a positive outlook based on the promises of God's Word. Hope can be defined as a quiet and steady expectation of good. It is an optimistic attitude that always chooses to see the best in life. It will not give way to depression and doubt, and self-pity. Romans 8:28 gives me every reason to be optimistic.

> And we know that all things work together for good to those who love God, to those who are the called according to His purpose. (NKJV)

You will find this verse popping up regularly in my story. When I focus on this truth that is mine as a child of God, knowing that He works all things together for my good, there is never any real reason to be downcast and pessimistic. That said, I am very aware that life can deal some pretty hard blows and make it very difficult to sustain an attitude of optimism. I must be ever on the alert with my helmet of hope and my garment of praise and my sword that is the Word of God, standing firm and ever ready to face the enemy head-on before he gets a stronghold over my mind, and thus, my life.

Deliverance through Identity and Inheritance

One of the symptoms of spiritual stagnation that inhibited my growth as a Christian was *ill-defined identity*, primarily due to my lack of knowledge and vague understanding concerning certain biblical truths. I knew that I was saved from an imminent eternity in hell and was assured of my salvation, but I was not fully aware of my true identity in Christ and what that meant for me here and now. As a result, I was not experiencing the victory that should have been mine over my inner struggles with negative thoughts and so on. I was left feeling depressed and sorry for myself.

Once I understood my true identity as a *child of God*, and what that means concerning the authority I have over the enemy, I began to experience victory over the darkness that hung over my life. Jesus took upon Himself all of my sins and burdens, all the negatives in my life, when He went to the cross on my behalf.

> Surely He has borne our **griefs** And carried our **sorrows**; Yet we esteemed Him stricken, smitten by God, and afflicted. But He was wounded for our **transgressions**, He was bruised for our **iniquities**; The chastisement **for our peace** was upon

Him, And by His stripes **we are healed** (Isaiah 53:4-5 NKJV). [Emphasis mine].

I am reminded of a beautiful song I have sung as a solo in church called *'The Day He Wore My Crown'*, made popular by Sandi Patty. On one occasion, I introduced it to the congregation by reminding them that the day Jesus wore the crown of thorns, when He hung on the cross at Calvary, was the day a great exchange took place. His crown of thorns was meant for me. I was the one who deserved to wear it. I was deserving of punishment for my sins, not Jesus, who had never sinned in His life.

Not only did He wear my crown of thorns that day, but it was as if He actually removed His crown of glory, being the sinless Son of God, and handed it to me as a gift. In accepting His gift, I received a new identity in Christ. The day I received my gift of salvation, which was given to me purely by the Grace of God and not through any merit of my own, I became a child of God. I was adopted into His family. Every kingdom treasure that belongs to God the Father and God the Son now belongs to me. The inheritance of Jesus became my inheritance on the day He wore my crown and gave me a new identity in Him. I stand in Christ, having been clothed in His righteousness, having the hope of Glory here and now.

For He made Him who knew no sin to be sin for us, that we might become the righteousness of God in Him (2 Corinthians 5:21 NKJV).

But God, who is rich in mercy, because of His great love with which He loved us, even when we were dead in trespasses, made us alive together with Christ (by grace you have been saved), and raised us up together, and made us sit together in the heavenly places in Christ Jesus, that in the ages to come He might show the exceeding riches of His grace in His kindness toward us in Christ Jesus (Ephesians 2:4-7 NKJV).

I do not have to wait until I get to heaven to claim my spiritual inheritance. My new life as an adopted child of God began the day I accepted Jesus as my Saviour, way back when I was only nine years old. Unfortunately, the significance of what it means to have a new identity in Christ did not begin to really sink in until much later in life.

You will recall that I have had a tendency to struggle with an inferiority complex over the years, particularly in my younger days, although I have to admit to still having my moments of falling into the trap of feeling like I do not quite measure up. Thankfully, my self-worth is not measured by my giftedness, talent, intellect, my beauty or lack thereof, or what I possess. Nor is it measured by whom I have perceived myself to be through many years of listening to the lies of Satan. My sense of personal worth comes from knowing who I am. I am a child of God. The God who created the universe is my Heavenly Father and my Heavenly Husband. He knows me and loves me intimately, and He calls me His own.

For many years, I perceived myself to be less than accepted by many of my peers, causing me to feel self-conscious and uncomfortable in their presence. I mistakenly thought that the source of my worth as a person was reliant on the acceptance of others. I was neglecting to see myself the way God sees me and, to that degree, have therefore suffered from a poor self-image. I did not grasp, nor understand, my true identity in Him.

I was unwittingly identifying with the first of God's earthly created sons, Adam. At my physical birth, I inherited his nature which has a tendency to come back and bite me. When Adam and Eve alienated themselves from God through sin, their sense of belonging and acceptance was lost. Ever since then, humanity has had an inbuilt need to belong and to be accepted by our peers, having lost our sense of self-worth. But, thankfully, the story does not end there.

As a spiritually born-again Christian, I now recognise who I am in Christ. I no longer identify with the first Adam but with the second and last Adam, Jesus. Not only did Jesus give me the gift of His identity the day He wore my crown, but He also gave me the gift of His Holy Spirit, who now dwells in me.

When I recognise myself as a newly born child of God, who is now seated at the right hand of God the Father with Christ, I am equipped to live out my salvation in all its fullness; claiming the promises of God as my inheritance, being an heir to God's kingdom through Christ Jesus.

> For as many as are led by the Spirit of God, these are the sons of God. For you did not receive the **spirit of bondage** again to fear, but you received the **Spirit of adoption** by whom we cry out, "Abba Father." The Spirit Himself bears witness with our spirit that **we are children of God**, and if children, then heirs –heirs of God and joint heirs with Christ, if indeed we suffer with Him, that we also may be glorified together (Romans 8:14-17 NKJV). [Emphasis mine].

Deliverance through the Power of the Holy Spirit and the Renewing of my Mind

But if the Spirit of Him who raised Jesus from the dead dwells in you, He who raised Christ from the dead will also **give life to your mortal bodies through His Spirit who dwells in you** (Romans 8:11 NKJV). [Emphasis mine].

When I *fully comprehend* that the same Holy Spirit who raised Christ from the dead dwells in me, I am empowered to overcome the enemy who vies to take control of my mind. When I place my faith in Christ, who *is* in me in the person of His Holy Spirit, and yield to Him daily, then my mind is gradually being renewed to be in keeping with God's perfect plan for my life.

I beseech you therefore, brethren, by the mercies of God, that **you present your bodies a living sacrifice**, holy, acceptable to God, which is your reasonable service. And do not be conformed to this world, but be transformed by the **renewing of your mind**, that you may prove what is that **good** and **acceptable** and **perfect** will of God (Romans 12:1-2 NKJV). [Emphasis mine].

When the Apostle Paul wrote the above passage in Romans 12, I assume he was speaking in the context of how it was for the Roman soldiers of that day. When the soldiers presented themselves to the Roman authorities, they literally handed themselves over to the care of the commanding officers, relinquishing all they had to those who would take charge of them. It may have been an obligation, but it was also the choice of the soldiers to do so. They would choose to get up in the morning and present themselves to those in authority, whose responsibility it was to feed them and clothe them and tell them what they needed to do.

This is an illustration of how the Holy Spirit takes over as my provider, my leader, and my guide when I choose to present myself to Him as a living sacrifice. In doing so, I yield to His authority over me and trust that He will take care of me.

To live a life of victory over depression and sin and over the pressures all around that constantly tempt me to conform to the standards of this world, I must offer my life to God daily. As an act of faith, I give myself over to the power of the Holy Spirit, believing that Christ now lives for me. My mortal body and flesh become a living sacrifice.

This is not a painful experience as the word 'sacrifice' implies. It is simply a matter of handing myself over to the care of another, believing by faith that I no longer live for myself but for Christ. In fact, *I* no longer live, but it is actually Christ who lives in and through me. In yielding to Him, I come under the sovereign authority and power of the Holy Spirit as my leader and guide.

> Therefore, if anyone is **in Christ,** he is a **new creation;** old things have passed away; behold, all things have become new (2 Corinthians 5:17 NKJV). [Emphasis mine].

> I have been crucified with Christ; It is no longer I who live, but **Christ lives in me**; and the life which I now live in the flesh **I live by faith in the Son of God**, who loved me and gave Himself for me (Galatians 2:20 NKJV). [Emphasis mine].

Deliverance through Positive Thinking

I have a teaching CD of a Christian psychologist who speaks about the mind being made up of neuron pathways. Each thought that goes into these neuron pathways is called a neuron chip. It has been scientifically proven that the chemical imbalance that occurs in the brain is mainly due to the mind being filled with neuron chips that are of a negative nature. In other words, negative thinking is a cause of depression. By focusing on positive thoughts instead of negative, my mind is gradually renewed. I am slowly but surely enabled to overcome depression.

> Finally, brethren, whatever things are true, whatever things are noble, whatever things are just, whatever things are pure, whatever things are lovely, whatever things are of good report, if there is any virtue and if there is anything praiseworthy – **meditate on these things** (Philippians 4:8 NKJV). [Emphasis mine].

Through biblical meditation, (which is a filling of one's mind as opposed to the New Age practice of emptying one's mind,) I saturate my mind with the truths and promises in God's Word, thinking and focusing on all things that are of a positive nature. In doing so, the negative neuron chips that have filled my neuron pathways are gradually replaced with positive neuron chips.

As soon as a negative thought enters my mind, I must take it captive before it becomes a stronghold. I need to recognise it for what it is, that it is a ploy by Satan to control my thoughts. It is imperative that I cast such negative thoughts out of my mind before they have a chance to take hold.

> For though we walk in the flesh, we do not war according to the flesh. For the weapons of our warfare are not carnal

but mighty in God for pulling down strongholds, casting down arguments and every high thing that exalts itself against the knowledge of God, **bringing every thought into captivity to the obedience of Christ.** (2 Corinthians 10:3-5 NKJV). [Emphasis mine].

For God has not given us a **spirit of fear**, but of power and of love and of a **sound mind** (2 Timothy 1:7 NKJV). [Emphasis mine].

Deliverance through Resting

You might cast your mind back to the vision I saw of a computer screen, in the middle of which was an icon with PREPARATION FOR DESTINATION written on it.

As I pondered over what I saw in my vision in the early hours, I decided to mentally click on the activator button on the computer screen. In my mind, I found myself entering God's throne room. Just as a computer is full of knowledge, it was as though I were entering into the dwelling place of God's omniscience, into the throne room of the all-knowing God. It was there that I laid down at His feet and **rested**, knowing that **He knew** what the future held and that **He was in control.**

From this experience, I began to learn what it truly means to **rest** in the Lord. Due to Nimali and Ben's relationship breakup, I felt burdened and weighed down with anxiety and depression. For a time, brief though it was at that point, I was able to relax in God's presence. As I lay there at His feet, I experienced a beautiful sense of relief as I handed my burdens over to Him. Although I did not know His will for the future concerning Nimali and Ben, I was able to relax in the knowledge that He was in control of their lives and mine.

My Sovereign God, the creator of the heavens and the earth, can see the big picture of my life. He knew everything about me, even before my mother conceived me in her womb. According to His Word, I know that **all** things work together for good to those who love the Lord. Not only does this knowledge give me every reason to be optimistic, but it also gives me every reason to **rest** in His love. I relax and surrender my life and the burdens that weigh me down into His control and care. This experience prompted me to turn the word rest into an acronym: R.E.S.T... Relax Entirely, Submit Totally.

When I *relax entirely* and *submit* my life *totally* to the Lord, I can *rest* in His love. I live my life from a place of victory over anxiety and depression instead of defeat. Entire surrender to Jesus is the secret of perfect rest.

> Come to Me, all you who labor and are heavy laden, and I will give you rest. Take My yoke upon you and learn from Me, for I am gentle and lowly in heart, and you will find rest for your souls. For My yoke is easy and My burden is light (Matthew 11:28-30 NKJV).

Deliverance through Abiding in Christ

When the light in my mind was switched on concerning the following passage of scripture, my whole outlook and attitude to life began to change. I began to feel liberated.

A friend of mine had given me a book called '*Abiding in Christ*' by Andrew Murray. It is based on the following passage where Jesus says:

> "I am the vine, and My Father is the vinedresser. Every branch in Me that does not bear fruit He takes away; and every branch that bears fruit He prunes, that it may bear more fruit. You are already clean because of the word which I have spoken to you.

Abide in Me, and I in you. As the branch cannot bear fruit of itself, unless it abides in the vine, neither can you, unless you abide in Me.

"I am the vine, you are the branches. He who abides in Me, and I in him, bears much fruit; for without Me you can do nothing. If anyone does not abide in Me, he is cast out as a branch and is withered; and they gather them and throw them into the fire, and they are burned. If you abide in Me, and My words abide in you, you will ask what you desire, and it shall be done for you. By this My Father is glorified, that you bear much fruit; so you will be My disciples.

"As the Father loved Me, I also have loved you; continue in My love. If you keep My commandments, you will abide in My love, just as I have kept My Father's commandments and abide in His love.

"These things I have spoken to you, that My joy may remain in you, and that your joy may be full. This is My commandment, that you love one another as I have loved you" (John 15:1-12 NKJV).

I had read this passage many times over the years, but I had never fully grasped what it truly means to *abide in Christ*. Once again, I had succumbed to the spiritually stagnant symptom of *ill-defined identity*, in that I did not fully understand, nor comprehend, my position in Christ.

I spent many years *striving* through my own burdensome efforts to be more like Jesus, trying to reflect His character. Instead, I should have been simply resting and abiding in Him, trusting Him to produce the fruits of His Spirit in and through me. 'Toiling on, toiling on, we will labour till the Master comes' seems to be the mindset of many Christians, including myself, until recent years, when I read this book by Andrew Murray.

NEWS FLASH!!

When it comes to being like Christ, *we do not have to do anything*, according to the passage above. That is, nothing except stay attached to the Vine. The analogy of the vine and the branches is liberating. It was as if a huge burden had been lifted off my shoulders when I first realised that it is not up to me to try to change my sinful fleshly ways. I cannot reflect the character and nature of Jesus through my own fleshly efforts. It is not up to me to produce the fruits of the Spirit in my life. According to this passage, the onus is all on Jesus. My only responsibility is to remain in complete union with Him. As the Father is in Christ and Christ is in the Father, so too is Christ in me and I in Christ. This mystery is so profound that I find it difficult to put it into words. Yet, it is a mystery that all believers would do well to fully grasp and understand in order to live a victorious life of empowerment.

It was in connection with the parable of the vine that Jesus first used the expression "Abide in Me". He demonstrates to us the intimate union to which He invites us. The connection between the vine and the branch is a living one. The life, the sap, the fatness, and the fruitfulness of the branch are only possible because of its attachment to the vine. The union is so close that each is completely reliant on the other to fulfil their purpose. Without the vine, the branch can do nothing. So too, without the branch, the vine can do nothing. The glory and fruitfulness of the vine is revealed through the branch. The branch can only produce fruit to the extent that it remains in complete union with the vine, receiving nourishment and empowerment through its life-giving sap.

And so it is with me and my relationship with Jesus. What a beautiful illustration of the Father's heart is this parable of the vine and the branches. Note again what Jesus said in John 15:11.

> As the Father loved Me, I also have loved you; abide in My love.
> If you keep my commandments, you will abide in My love, just

as I have kept My Father's commandments and abide in His love.

These things I have spoken to you, that **My joy may remain in you**, and that **your joy may be full**." (NKJV) [Emphasis mine].

Not only will my life be prosperous and bear fruit as I abide in Christ, but the *'spirit of heaviness'* that vies to hold me captive to depression is overcome and replaced with His joy. To truly experience the *fullness of joy*, I need only remain in complete union with Christ and His abiding Spirit, basking in His love and His everlasting embrace.

Another one of my acronyms: A.B.I.D.E ... Always Being In Divine Embrace.

PART IV

Spiritual Menu

CHAPTER 8

The Blessing of Grace

Ever since I can remember, we as a family would always 'say grace' before a meal. My parents encouraged it and I still practice it today. It may be a simple prayer when I sit down to eat, saying, "Thank you Lord for this food". When we get together with extended family to share a meal, we always first gather around and 'say grace'.

What does it mean to 'say grace?' Wikipedia tells me that… *'A grace is a short prayer or thankful phrase said before or after eating. The term most commonly refers to Christian traditions. Some traditions hold that grace and thanksgiving imparts a blessing which sanctifies the meal. In English, reciting such a prayer is sometimes referred to as "saying grace"'.*

We will share a 'meal' in the next few chapters. I have written of my experiences in discovering God's 'spiritual menu' of metaphorical food that, when appropriated into my life daily, would slowly but surely cause a 'shift' in my spiritually stagnant state.

As we embark on this meal, it is only appropriate to address the topic of grace. That is, God's grace! God's undeserving favour toward His creation, the greatest blessing made freely available to us if we only accept it by faith. Just as we speak grace over our food, a blessing of sanctification that the food would nourish our bodies, so too, God's grace is a source of blessing and sanctification to us both physically and spiritually.

I am very much a work in progress in need of much grace. So, too, has been this project of writing my story. You may be aware that this edition you are reading is my third. After releasing the second edition, I sensed that the Lord would have me change the title. I grappled with this as He had given me the original title in a vision, and I didn't feel that it was my place to make major changes to something I believed was of the Lord. Nonetheless, I sought confirmation as I was unsettled about what He would have me do. It came to me in a dream like this:

I found myself standing in the kitchen of our previous home in Taree. As I stood there, I was conscious that the house had been substantially renovated, including the reconstruction of a completely new roof. Yet, as I looked up at the ceiling of this renovated home, I could see water leaking all around the cornices and dripping down the walls.

At that point, I woke up. I understood that this dream was relevant to my book. Just as the house in my dream had been renovated, my book has also undergone some fairly major revisions. In my dream, I looked up, my attention particularly drawn to the new roof my husband had redesigned and constructed on our house. As I considered its relevance, the Lord confirmed that my book was to receive a 'new roof' in the form of a new title. I was relieved that I was on the right track in suspecting the Lord would have me make further changes to the book, but I was intrigued by the leaks. So as I was standing at my kitchen sink one morning, having a chat with the Lord, I asked Him, "What's causing the leaks?" In His still, small voice, He replied, "*Gaps! Fill in the gaps!*"

The Grace Gap

I must confess, in previous editions of my story, I neglected to address, in-depth, the most important foundational truth that is at the heart of my faith as a Christian. That is the all-important and non-negotiable gift of God's grace in my life. Without the gift of grace, I am nothing. *Grace* is the all-important adhesive that fills in the gaps of my story, my journey through life. It is the substance that holds and sustains me through the good and the bad things that come my way. It is my very source of salvation.

Grace would have no need or purpose for existence except for there being an object or reason for which it is applied or granted. All that is not perfect in this degenerating world needs God's grace.

God's grace is usually defined as undeserved favour. I am forever grateful for God's grace, mercy and favour in my life. Yet, I can't help but think there is so much more to understand about grace than what initially comes to mind. God's grace is so intrinsic to life itself that I find it difficult to express the depth of its meaning and significance. Without God's grace, the world and all that exists would not be sustained. It is God's grace that creates and sustains life itself. He holds the earth, the sun, the moon and every heavenly being in their rightful place in His all-sustaining hand, all due to His favour, His grace. If He were to remove His hand of grace, the world we know would be obliterated. It would cease to exist. How so reliant we are on God's grace, not only in this life but for all eternity.

Only by grace am I destined for an eternity with God, rather than an eternity that does not even bear thinking about if God were not in it. Without knowing God's grace, His favour, His goodness, life is not worth living.

The only way we become eligible to receive God's gift of grace and favour is through acknowledging our need for it. God, who *is* goodness and love, can have nothing to do with anyone or anything that falls short of His goodness, perfection, and holiness. God can't tolerate evil because it goes against all that He is.

As an imperfect human, I must first acknowledge my need for forgiveness for my sins, my shortcomings, and imperfections before a perfect God to receive His favour. It is impossible to come before a Holy and perfect God in my unworthiness, *but*, for God and His gift of grace and favour.

In His goodness and love for His creation, God made a way for you and I to be forgiven for our sins and shortcomings, all by His Grace. He made a way through His only begotten Son, Jesus, so that all who believe in Him are made *righteous* in God's sight as newly created beings. Through belief in the death and resurrection of Jesus, who took upon Himself the penalty for my sin, which is death, God the Father forgives me of all my sins and cleanses me from all unrighteousness. By faith in God's promise of forgiveness, by accepting His gift of grace that I do not deserve, He declares me blameless. I am now justified before a righteous judge, as if I had never sinned. I can't help but sing, *'Amazing grace, how sweet the sound that saved a wretch like me. I once was lost, but now I am found. I was blind, but now I see.'*

Where would I be without the grace of almighty God? I would be lost. I would not only be lost and floundering around, looking for purpose and direction in this life on earth, but I would be lost for all eternity. Praise God that He made a way! Praise God for His undeserved favour toward a world unworthy to be called anything but filthy rags before a Holy sovereign God. Yet, He loves us so much! He longs to have fellowship with us. He created you and me for this very purpose. That He would know us, and we would know and love and serve Him with all of our being. And so He grants to us His gift of grace.

A gift is of no benefit to anyone unless it is gratefully received and appropriated, using its benefits. I reluctantly admit that I have not 'appropriated' grace well! The blessings and benefits available to me as God's child are immeasurable. Yet, until I come to the point where I daily walk in the light of His grace, knowing the blessings of God's rest and peace, ceasing from striving in costly works of the flesh, my life will not be all as God intended in granting His gift of grace. I must learn to put off fleshly habits of fear, anxiety, self-focus, and the need for affirmation and acceptance of others apart from God Himself. The all-sustaining grace of God my Heavenly Father, is all I need to truly walk in power and strength and acceptance as His adopted child. I can do nothing without Him, and all my works and efforts to please are for naught!

> For by grace you have been saved through faith, and that not
> of yourselves; it is the gift of God, not of works, lest anyone

should boast. For we are His workmanship, created in Christ Jesus for good works, which God prepared beforehand that we should walk in them. (Ephesians 2:8-9 NKJV)

I have tended to try to work out my salvation in my own strength. I am guilty of 'feeling guilty' when I feel I have fallen short of God's plan. I neglect to walk in grace, knowing that God loves me just as I am. My Heavenly Father loves and accepts me, even in my failings. As for trying to work out God's will and plan for my life in my strength and ability, I am told in the above passage of scripture that God, in His grace, had my life all planned out long before I was even born. I am not saved *by* good works but *for* good works. The Lord knows exactly what He would have me do for Him as I journey through this life. I just need to stay in tune with His Spirit so that I might walk out my purpose in His strength. It's time I learn to walk in grace well. To relax in the knowledge that God has redeemed me from all that keeps me bound in bondage, knowing that He has conquered death through Jesus and, in Him, I find my strength and sufficiency to live life well and abundantly.

And He said to me, "My grace is sufficient for you, for my strength is found perfect in weakness." Therefore most gladly I

> boast in my infirmities, that the power of Christ may rest upon me. (2 Corinthians 12:9 NKJV)

What a blessing to know that God supplies me with enough grace to face every situation that comes my way. Grace for facing illness and financial need. Grace for my lack of wisdom and social skills. Grace for every trial and challenge imaginable. Almighty God has granted me access to His strength to cope in all circumstances. All I need is to believe it to be so through faith. Grace is accessed through faith and submission. Praise God for His mercy to a helpless and dying world, consumed by evil and ultimately destined for death. God, in His mercy and grace, sent His Son into the world to die in our place. Through faith in Jesus, we are redeemed and sanctified, set apart to be holy, knowing the fullness of life in Christ for all eternity.

> But God, who is rich in mercy, because of His great love with which He loved us, even when we were dead in trespasses, made us alive together with Christ (by grace you have been saved), and raised us up together, and made us sit together in the heavenly places in Christ Jesus, that in the ages to come He might show the exceeding riches of His grace in His kindness toward us in Christ Jesus (Ephesians 2:4-7 NKJV).

A well known acronym: G.R.A.C.E.   God's Riches At Christ's Expense. Amazing Grace!

◇◇◇◇◇◇◇◇

Let's say grace for the meal ahead, shall we?

Thank you Lord, for the 'food' we will receive in the following chapters. Bless it to us, sanctifying us as we partake and appropriate what you have prepared for us to do and be. Set us apart to be holy as you are Holy. In Jesus' precious name, we pray! Amen.

CHAPTER 9

Apply the Butter to the Bread

'It sounds like perfectionism!' This was a comment made during one of our church home-group discussions. It was mentioned in the study material we were looking at that one of God's objectives for His creation is excellence. By comparing myself with that which is excellent in God's eyes, I can see that I fall short of His desires and objectives for me as His created being. This was not always the case as far as His creation was concerned. When God created the world, He took great delight in seeing that it was good. It was excellent. In Genesis 1:26-27 God said:

> "Let Us make man in Our image, according to Our likeness; let them have dominion over the fish of the sea, over the birds of the air, and over the cattle, over all the earth and every creeping thing that creeps on the earth." So God created man in His own image; in the image of God He created him; male and female He created them. (NKJV)

God's intent in creating man and woman in His image was that we would be a reflection of His very likeness and being, to state the obvious. That is not to say, of course, that we can by any means be *equal* with God. Lucifer thought he was of equal status with God, and we know what happened to him. He was cast out of heaven, along with his admiring angels, destined for eternal condemnation in hell.

No. Equality with God does not even bear thinking about. Yet just as God is Holy, His objective when creating humanity was that we would *be holy*. God created humanity with His own attributes to equip us to defeat Satan, who was already residing in our earthly realm awaiting his final demise. Satan's quest, in the meantime, is to rule over the earth. In the very beginning, humanity was given authority by God to subdue all created things so that all things may be subject to His sovereign rule.

In His sovereignty, God gave Adam and Eve freewill, which meant they could choose their own destiny. They could choose to heed God's instruction by refraining from eating of the tree that God forbade them to eat of in the Garden of Eden. Or they could choose to disregard His instruction. Had they been left to their own devices, perhaps all would have been well. Or maybe not!

As it turned out, Satan entered the Garden and deceived Adam and Eve by whetting their fleshly appetite, suggesting that they could be of equal status with God if they ate the fruit of the forbidden tree. Adam and Eve fell to this temptation, believing Satan's lies. They fell from their place of honour by disobeying God's instruction, causing the theme of God's excellence to be severed. By coming into agreement with Satan, having fallen victim to his deceptive words instead of heeding God's voice, they effectively forfeited their God-given authority to rule over the planet as perfect and holy ambassadors of God. Most unfortunately for us, the rule fell somewhat surreptitiously into the evil hands of Satan.

The perfect intimate union between a Holy God and His creation was thwarted. Yet, God's purpose and intent to bring heaven's rule to earth remains to this day, as affirmed by the Lord's prayer: 'Your kingdom come, Your will be done on earth *as it is in heaven*.' Heaven and all its attributes are perfect. The Garden of Eden and its occupants *were perfect* until sinful man caused it to fall into corruption.

It was only through the coming of Christ that God's perfect plan for a holy kinship was put back on track. Jesus paid the penalty for the sins of humanity, thereby claiming back that which was lost, being the authority to rule over the planet.

As I have already stated, God's intent remains the same as it was in the beginning. His Bride (the Church) is empowered again through Christ to defeat Satan, to go about God's business of bringing the earth and its occupants into subjection to His sovereign rule.

This is all very well, but there was just one problem. I do not know about you, but for many years, I did not feel very victorious when it came to defeating Satan. I was (and still am) far from feeling anything close to being holy. I knew that I was fully justified in the eyes of God through my faith in Jesus and His redeeming sacrifice, but I was still feeling defeated and was falling short of being the powerful conqueror God would have me be.

Getting back to the comment made at our home-group Bible study about God's objective that His Bride be holy, I sensed a degree of scepticism in what was said. The comment implied that the study material seemed to be leaning toward the doctrine of perfectionism.

Further discussion followed. The opinion of most was that it seems impossible that we could ever fully reach the standard of excellence the study was suggesting we aspire to. All agreed that as Christians, we need to be looking to Jesus as our example and *try* to be more like Him. (The emphasis is on 'try'.) Yet, there was a strong vibe coming through the discussion that we could never achieve such a high standard of excellence because ... *we are still living in the flesh*!

For many years I have battled with my fleshly carnal nature, succumbing to my spiritually stagnant condition. I have constantly striven to be a better person, trying to live up to the expectations that are mine as a Christian, but I seem to fail miserably. I certainly relate to what the Apostle Paul says in Romans 7:18-19:

> I know that nothing good lives in me, that is, in my sinful nature. For I have the desire to do what is good, but I cannot carry it out. For what I do is not the good I want to do; no, the evil I do not want to do – this I keep doing. (NIV)

I am sure we can all relate to this. I have always presumed I would never fully reach my goal of becoming holy until I reach heaven. The argument many Christians use to condone our weakness in the flesh is that if the Apostle Paul, who was an amazing man of God, struggled with the flesh, then what hope do we have?

I struggle with my fleshly inclinations, no doubt about that! I have wondered, though, to what extent this ought to be the case. I am a born-again believer in the death and resurrection of Jesus, whose *flesh* was crucified on my behalf, thereby conquering the *power* of sin and death. Would it not be reasonable to assume that His intent and purpose was to *free* me from the *power* that the flesh has over me in the here and now, and not just when I get to heaven?

Paul, in his statement above, referred to the lack of victory we have over sin. That is, while ever we are slaves to the law and the flesh. Paul was explaining to the Romans that without the law, we would not even be aware that there is such a thing as sin. He says in Romans 7:7:

> What shall we say then? Is the law sin? Certainly not! On the contrary, I would not have known sin except through the law. For I would not have known covetousness unless the law had said, *"You shall not covet."* (NKJV)

Paul says in the previous verse 6:

> But now we have been delivered from the law, **having died to what we were held by**, so that we should serve **in the newness of the Spirit** and not in the oldness of the letter. (NKJV) [Emphasis mine].

Paul goes on to say in Romans 7:24-25:

O wretched man that I am! Who will deliver me from this body of death? **I thank God – through Jesus Christ our Lord!** (NKJV) [Emphasis mine].

Paul continues in Romans 8:1-15:

There is therefore now no condemnation to those who are in Christ Jesus, **who do not walk according to the flesh, but according to the Spirit.** For the law of the Spirit of life in Christ Jesus has made me **free** from the law of sin and death. For what the law could not do in that it was weak through the flesh, God did by sending His own Son in the likeness of sinful flesh, on account of sin: **He condemned sin in the flesh**, that the righteous requirement of the law might be fulfilled in us **who do not walk according to the flesh** but **according to the Spirit.** For those who live according to the flesh **set their minds on the things of the flesh**, but those who live **according to the Spirit, the things of the Spirit.** For to be **carnally minded is death**, but to be s**piritually minded** is **life** and **peace**. Because the carnal mind is enmity against God;

for it is not subject to the law of God, nor indeed can be. So then, those who are in the flesh cannot please God.

But you are not in the flesh but in the Spirit, if indeed the Spirit of God dwells in you. Now if anyone does not have the Spirit of Christ, he is not His. And if Christ is in you, the body is dead because of sin, but the Spirit is life because of righteousness. **But if the Spirit of Him who raised Jesus from the dead dwells in you, He who raised Christ from the dead will also give life to your mortal bodies through His Spirit who dwells in you.**

Therefore, brethren, we are debtors -- not to the flesh, to live according to the flesh. For if you live according to the flesh you will die; but if **by the Spirit you put to death the deeds of the body**, you will live. For as many as are **led by the Spirit of God,** these are sons of God. **For you did not receive the spirit of bondage** again to fear, but you received the **Spirit of adoption** by whom we cry out, "Abba Father." (NKJV) [Emphasis mine].

Paul thanks God in Romans 7:24-25 that he - and we also - have been delivered from *this body of death* through Jesus Christ our Lord.

The Spirit of God almighty who dwells in me will give me victory over the flesh as I yield to His power; when I offer my carnal, fleshly body to Him as a living sacrifice every day. This is an act of faith, and I have to believe it to be true, that He will lead, guide, and empower me in all that I do. It is not through my own efforts that I might pertain to holiness, but only by yielding to Christ and being completely reliant on Him.

As far as my salvation and standing in the eyes of God the Father are concerned, I stand before Him as a righteous daughter. Having been saved from the consequences of sin through Christ, I no longer come under the rule of condemnation and eternal judgement. Nonetheless, I am still very much in need of a considerable degree of reformation, restoration, and refining to take place so that I might fully reflect God's being as the perfect Bride, clothed in 'The Beauty of Holiness'.

As daunting as it may be, I cannot ignore the several references in God's Word that indicate God's will and intent that His Bride *be holy* and *perfect*.

> ...but as He who called you is holy, you also be holy in all your conduct, because it is written, **"Be holy, for I am holy"** (1 Peter 1:15-16 NKJV). [Emphasis mine].

Whoever abides in Him **does not sin**. Whoever sins has neither seen Him nor known Him (1 John 3:6 NKJV). [Emphasis mine].

Therefore you shall **be perfect**, just as your Father in heaven is perfect (Matthew 5:48 NKJV). [Emphasis mine].

One day, I talked with a friend about God's intent that we as believers can attain His objective for us to be holy. In fact, it would seem that scripture alludes to the possibility that holiness is achievable simply because we have been instructed to *be* holy. I emphasised that this is not possible through any efforts of our own or through any amount of striving in the flesh, but only through intimate union with the Holy Spirit, relying on His power as He dwells in us.

My friend, on the other hand, was quite emphatic that *we still live in the flesh.* She believed we can never achieve such an objective in our earthly bodies, and to think one could possibly achieve perfection would only result in constant disappointment and self-condemnation. I understood where she was coming from, but I was not convinced by her argument.

Please do not misunderstand. I am not basing my thoughts on any misappropriated belief that I have reached the goal of achieving perfect holiness. Far from it, believe me! But I desire to avail myself and to be open to all that God has on offer to me in the hope of achieving *His objectives* in my life. Again, I relate to what the Apostle Paul says in Philippians 3:12-14:

> Not that I have already attained, or am already perfected; but I press on, that I may lay hold of that for which Christ Jesus has also laid hold of me. Brethren, I do not count myself to have apprehended; but one thing I do, forgetting those things which are behind and reaching forward to those things which are ahead, I press toward the goal for the prize of the upward call of God in Christ Jesus. (NKJV)

For most people, myself included, the idea of having to aspire to be holy and perfect is quite frightening because we perceive it to be totally out of our reach and unachievable. We think it means that you never do anything wrong, and that you never say anything wrong; you never make mistakes.

With considerable relief, I now understand that to be perfect, as defined in scripture, is to be spiritually mature or complete. Having grown from being infants in our faith to being grown-up sons and daughters, one might say.

In this light, the prospect of attaining holiness is perhaps not so daunting. At least, one would like to think so. The more we *mature* as Christians, the more one would suppose that the struggles we experience with the flesh should begin to dissipate. Yet this is not necessarily the case for some of us, or so it would seem.

I accepted Jesus as my Lord and Saviour at the age of nine, having been well-churched and grounded in the Word of God. One would expect by now that I would be maturing reasonably well in my growth as a Christian. Yet, even by the time I had reached my early fifties, having been a Christian for forty years, I was still very frustrated with my struggles with the flesh. Even to this day, I might add, I am very much a work in progress. Obviously, in my case at least, length in time does not necessarily equate to maturity when being a Christian. This continual struggle with the flesh caused me to believe that I was missing something in my walk with the Lord. I was spiritually stagnant, as it were, being spiritually aged as a Christian of many years, but still struggling with my fleshly carnal nature. I have been a slave to my flesh.

Jesus suffered on the cross so that I might be set free from the power that the flesh has over me. Why would He die to save me and set me free from the consequences of sin, only to have me struggle with my flesh for the rest of my life? I am not denying the fact that I will most definitely continue to experience trials in life. Yet, I can have victory over my struggles through *faith in* the power of Christ, whose resurrected body is now in me in the form of His Holy Spirit.

Why is it that many Christians, whom I would have considered reasonably mature in the faith, have this common mindset that the flesh has such power over us? Why is it that we believe we will never reach the standard of holiness that God would have us achieve as mature sons and daughters of the living God? In fostering such thoughts, I fear we are in danger of offending the Holy Spirit. Such thinking supposes that *our flesh* is *more powerful* than the *Holy Spirit* who dwells in us.

In the early hours of one morning, I expressed to the Lord my frustration concerning this mindset that is prevalent among many Christians, including myself. It seems as though there is a blockage in such thinking, as though we cannot comprehend the reality of the power that lives in us in the person of the Holy Spirit.

As I was laying there with my eyes closed, the Holy Spirit impressed upon my mind a picture or vision:

I saw a drinking glass containing a portion of butter. The glass was tilted as if someone was drinking the butter.

I wondered about this for a little while, contemplating its significance. I concluded that the butter represents the blockage occurring in the hearts and minds of many sincere and very dedicated Christians, none more so than myself. God revealed to me through this impression that I had been enjoying drinking the 'milk' of God's Word for so many years that it had become over-processed and turned into *butter*. The butter represents *a slave-to-the-flesh mentality* that has hindered my growth as a Christian, resulting in spiritual stagnancy.

Ever since the age of nine, I knew the Holy Spirit lived in my heart and that He would help me become a better person. This doctrine had been instilled into me over many years, yet I still did not feel empowered in my daily walk as a Christian. I loved the Lord God with all my heart. I had been fully dedicated to serving Him for many years. I was well-grounded in the truth of God's Word. One would have liked to think that I had progressed *beyond* feeding on the *milk* of God's Word. Yet, in all my sincerity, it is apparent that I was still an *infant* as far as my Christian maturity was concerned.

When addressing the Corinthian Church in the first book of Corinthians, chapter three, Paul referred to them as *infants* because they were not yet spiritually healthy and mature. They still needed to be fed *milk* because they were not quite ready for solid food. His reasoning for this was that their lives were still reflective of their carnal nature. *They were still living under the power and influence of the flesh.* There is also reference to this seeming lack of maturity of the believers in Hebrews 5:12-13.

> For though by this time you ought to be teachers, you need someone to teach you again the first principles of the oracles of God; and you have come to need milk and not solid food. For everyone who partakes only of milk is unskilled in the word of righteousness, for he is a babe. (NKJV)

Though I should have been mature in my faith after many years of being a Christian, I was still a babe. I was still living according to my fleshly carnal nature and consequently, I became spiritually stagnant, unable to grow and move forward in my faith.

I am so grateful that God gave me a hunger for more of Him. He is slowly but surely taking me beyond drinking milk and the *mindset* that has blocked my spiritual growth and progress as a Christian. He has given me an appetite for the more solid food available to me *in Christ, the Bread of life.*

I Need to Apply the Butter to the Bread!

In John chapter six, Jesus said:

Most assuredly, I say to you, Moses did not give you the bread from heaven, but My Father gives you the true bread from heaven. For the bread of God is He who comes down from heaven and **gives life to the world** (John 6:32-33 NKJV).

I am the living bread that came down from heaven. If anyone eats of this bread, he will live forever. **This bread is my flesh, which I will give for the life of the world** (John 6:51 NIV).

Most assuredly, I say to you, unless you eat the flesh of the Son of Man and drink his blood, **you have no life in you**. Whoever eats My flesh and drinks My blood has eternal life, and I will raise him up at the last day. For My flesh is food indeed, and My blood is drink indeed. **He who eats My flesh and drinks My blood abides in Me, and I in him**. As the living Father sent Me, and I live because of the Father, so **he who feeds on Me will live because of Me. This is the bread which came down from heaven** - not as your fathers ate the manna, and are dead. **He who eats this bread will live forever** (John 6:53-58 NKJV). [Emphasis mine].

So, how does Jesus give me His flesh as bread to eat? To eat living bread is to accept Christ into my life and *become united with Him*. I am united with Christ in two ways:

- By believing in His death (*the sacrifice of His flesh*) and His resurrection. By recognising that His flesh was crucified on my behalf and that He rose again to new life for me, thereby conquering the power that my old flesh had over me.
- By depending on His teaching for my guidance, being united with and trusting in the Holy Spirit for power.

The key to empowerment as a Christian is not *effort* but *union*! By being united with Christ and entirely trusting in the power of His Holy Spirit, I no longer put my trust in the power of the flesh.

The Great Exchange

God's remedy for sin is death by execution. God required that sin could only be atoned for through the shedding of blood through a sacrifice. Under the Old Testament law, sins were *temporarily* forgiven by sacrificing a perfect lamb. Under the new covenant, sins are *permanently* forgiven through Jesus' sacrifice. God required the blood of a *perfect human* to be shed for the atonement of sins to be perfect and complete. On the cross at Calvary, a great exchange took place. When Jesus was executed on the cross for the atonement of my sins, my flesh was crucified with Jesus. Therefore, my flesh no longer has any claim over me.

> I have been crucified with Christ; **it is no longer I who live, but Christ lives in me;** and the life which I now live in the flesh **I live by faith in the Son of God**, who loved me and gave Himself for me (Galatians 2:20 NKJV). [Emphasis mine].

I knew that I had received the Holy Spirit into my heart at the point of repentance and conversion to the faith. I knew it to be true. Yet, I had not learned to appropriate this knowledge into my life in such a way that I actually experienced the power that was in me. I was *trying* to be perfect, all in my own striving and strength!

I am learning to change my way of thinking to the truth of what *has already* changed. The truth is that *I no longer live.* It is Christ the Bread of life who gives me new life and power!

I *'apply the butter to the Bread'* by taking all I have learned over the years and appropriate it into my life so that it becomes more than just a theory and sound theology. I must wake up every morning and set my mind on God, presenting myself to Him and believing *by faith* that He will now take control of all that happens to me through the day. Then the Holy Spirit can begin His work of refining by shaping and moulding me to be the perfect (complete and mature) vessel that God created me to be. In submitting my life to His control, I am enabled to function as God intended. I begin to fulfil His objectives for my life. I am far from perfect, but I am learning that it is possible to live in victory over the power of the flesh; when I put my faith in Christ and submit to His Spirit who *is* in me!

Jesus is My Example

Jesus was entirely man and perfectly complete or holy. He was, and is, God incarnate. Jesus is, and always will be, God. Yet it would seem that He chose to set aside His 'God-power' while here on this earth to become fully man. I find it challenging to get my head around this, yet it is substantiated in scripture. Jesus said in John 5:19: '*...the Son can do nothing of Himself....*' He was reliant on the abiding union He knew with His Father and the Holy Spirit.

For many years I believed that Jesus was able to go about doing the many miracles, signs and wonders He performed simply because He was God. I thought that in His human-ness, He retained enough of His 'God-ness' (for want of a better word) so that He was able to do supernatural things. I believed that as a human being, He still retained enough of His 'God-power' so that He could overcome temptation and thereby be free from sin. I see now that this is not the case. (I suspect that some may prefer to challenge me on this, but please hear me out.)

Jesus was, in actual fact, fully and completely human while He walked on this earth. He was tempted with the flesh just as we are tempted with the flesh, yet He did not sin. How did He manage to do this?

Jesus was empowered because He knew who He was. He knew His true identity. He knew He was God's child, God's only begotten Son. He was empowered through an intimate relationship with His Father. He was empowered because He knew that His Father was in Him, and He was in the Father. It was His faith in this truth and reality that enabled Him to fulfil His calling. Jesus would often refer to Himself as the 'Son of Man' as if to affirm that He was living and functioning in this earthly realm as one of us.

Yes, Jesus was the third person in the Trinity. I most certainly am not refuting this truth. Jesus had not given up His divinity, only His right to operate from within it. He was the only begotten Son of God, yet He was functioning entirely as a human being.

When Jesus was baptised in the River Jordan, the heavens opened, and the Holy Spirit came and *rested on Him*. The voice of His Father was heard to say,

"This is My beloved Son, in whom I am well pleased" (Matthew 3:17 NKJV). The Father found favour in His Son!

Apart from the obvious, that Jesus was God's beloved Son, why did God find such favour in Jesus at that point in time, considering that He hadn't yet commenced His ministry? What was it about Jesus that pleased the Father so much?

I believe God's favour was upon Him because of the close and intimate union Jesus had known with His Father over His younger and growing years. He grew and matured in age and in relationship with His Father and was well-grounded in the scriptures from a young age. Jesus had attained a maturity that brought Him in line with His Father's goodwill and pleasure. It was the Father's good pleasure to give Jesus the Kingdom. Perhaps Jesus, as the Son of Man, proved Himself worthy in keeping with the Hebrew customs, as 30 is the age Hebrew men took over their father's business. With His baptism, Jesus was affirming His will and commitment to take over His Father's kingdom. Father God gave His 'kiss of approval' by sending His Spirit to anoint and enable Jesus to do what He was sent to do.

God the Father and God the Son, along with God the Holy Spirit, had been in perfect union and relationship from the beginning of time. Still, it was at this point in His earthly life, as the Holy Spirit now *rested upon* Him, that Jesus' *supernatural ministry* began with power. Jesus was enabled to go about doing the work He was called to do because He heard His Father's voice affirming His favour. At that point, His true identity was confirmed, and He was anointed with the Holy Spirit's power.

This realisation gives me hope. As an adopted child of God through His saving grace, knowing my new and true identity in Christ, I am called to be an ambassador of Jesus. I am called to follow His example. He commissioned me to go into all the world and to do as He did. Jesus said in John 14:12 that His followers would do even greater things than He did. YIKES! He re-commissioned you and me to do as God our creator authorised Adam and Eve to do in the beginning: to go about the business of establishing His kingdom here on earth. I am the first to admit that this is a daunting prospect, yet I can only assume that Jesus would not assign me to a task that He did not consider to be achievable.

Jesus tells His disciples in John 14:16 that after His ascension to heaven, the Father would send another helper in the person of the Holy Spirit. He would abide with us forever. He now dwells **with us** and is **in us**. What a fantastic promise. We simply must believe it to be true.

As Christ is in the Father and the Father is in Christ, so too, Christ is in me, and I am in Christ. I abide in Him, knowing an intimate union with

His Holy Spirit. As I give mindful attention to His Word and appropriate it into my life, I am empowered to be an overcomer. I am empowered to live in victory over the strongholds of Satan and my fleshly inclinations instead of defeat.

There is no denying that I am living in a fallen fleshly body that is warring against me, willing me to constantly fall short of God's standard of excellence. But surely, the power of the Holy Spirit who has taken up residence in me is far greater than the power of my *'old man'* who would seek to rear 'his' ugly head. Paul stated that:

> Our old man was crucified with Him, that the body of sin might be done away with, that we should no longer be slaves to sin (Romans 6:6 NKJV).

I will repeat it, 'I am far from perfect!' However, it is my sincere desire to daily put off the old man and put on the new who is Christ in me in the person of His Holy Spirit. By submitting my life fully to Him, being reliant on His enabling power, I can be victorious over the power of the flesh. As I 'apply the butter to the Bread,' I am released from the mindset that has held me captive as an infant in Christ. The ever-abiding power of the Holy Spirit enables me to apply the truths of sound doctrine that I have learned over the years and actually appropriate them into my life. I am being transformed as an adopted daughter of God into His very likeness. He is slowly but surely refining me to be the person He purposed me to be, and that is holy, just as He is Holy.

Now, is anyone craving a good feed of meat and vegies?

CHAPTER 10

Place the Meat on the Altar

Worship in Song

Oh come, let us sing to the LORD! Let us shout joyfully to the Rock of our salvation. Let us come before *His presence with thanksgiving; Let us shout joyfully to Him with psalms (Psalm 95:1-2 NKJV).*

As a young child, the love of singing was instilled in me, having been raised in a musical family. It has been an enjoyable and vital part of my entire life, especially as part of my church life. The singing of hymns and spiritual songs is an integral means of worshipping our God. Sadly, the very thing that should bring unity in the Church body can sometimes cause division. I had grown up in a generation where traditional hymns and choruses were the typical styles of music when I was younger. Now I enjoy the more modern contemporary songs and music as well as the older and modern-day hymns.

Our congregation is made up of an extensive range of age groups. This indicates that our Church is reasonably healthy, catering to the needs of people of all ages. However, this can have its issues due to the vast array of preferences regarding the style of music we utilise for worship in our Sunday services. Our Church has not been immune to this particular issue. There have been heated discussions in the past during church members' meetings, due to some people feeling that their music preferences were not catered to.

I have asked myself: *'Is it reasonable to expect to cater to everyone's preferences when it comes to music and worship in church?'* I would like to think that the answer to this question is *'yes*!'

On the other hand, should it be *necessary* to cater to everyone's preferences? I'm not so sure. I'm not sure that we ought to be so *reliant* on a particular style of music to truly enter into worship and spiritual communion with God. However, I accept that certain types of music are more conducive to worship than others for most individuals.

I confess these inconclusive ramblings have come about due to my having had the experience several years ago of entering into a discussion with another person on this topic which, I am sorry to say, became a little heated due to differences of opinion. Thankfully, it ended in love as we agreed to disagree.

I came away from this experience feeling quite shaken up and offended. It had been implied that *one* could not possibly worship God through the modern-day songs that we sing in church. I took offence to this, as I find many modern contemporary songs quite conducive to worship.

I went to bed with this incident on my mind. Such conflict over something that is so vital in our Christian experience disturbed me. I woke up the next morning still thinking about it, wondering what the solution is to this issue that can cause division in our churches.

I earnestly came before the Lord seeking His counsel, allowing Him the opportunity to speak to me if He so desired. In the stillness of the early morning hour, the Holy Spirit impressed upon my mind the following picture or dream:

I found myself in a butcher's shop. Quite a few people were waiting at the counter as the butcher randomly handed out various cuts of 'meat' to each person. The people receiving the meat didn't get to choose what they wanted. Nor did they complain about what they received. They simply accepted what they were given.

This image left my mind as quickly as it came. I briefly considered what the Lord would have me derive from this dream, concluding its meaning to be quite obvious:

Each cut or piece of meat represents the different styles of music we have 'handed to us' at church. The 'types of meat' are many and varied, yet they all serve the same purpose. They are songs of praise freely offered to us to enrich our spiritual appetite as we offer them back to God in worship. The 'meat' we are served may not be the preferred cut or portion we may choose for ourselves. It may not be according to our personal taste. Yet, as we relinquish our personal preferences and graciously accept what is given, we, in turn, give God the honour He deserves. We offer back to Him our 'meat' as a 'sacrifice of praise.'

I wonder whether most of us have been guilty at some point of having rejected the *meat* offered to us in worship. We all have varying tastes when it comes to music. The Lord has challenged me through this experience to check my own attitude concerning this issue. When I come to church with a genuine desire to serve the Lord by worshipping Him through music and song, I need to be open to accepting the 'meat' that is freely offered to me, as long as it is pleasing and honouring to God. As I come with a thankful heart and an attitude of submission, the music and the words of the songs contribute to drawing me into God's presence, helping to satisfy my hunger for more of Him. I can know an intimate union with my Heavenly Husband, His Holy Spirit drawing near to me as I draw near to Him.

As I took some time to consider what the Lord had placed on my heart concerning worship, I was reminded that as a small child, I was very picky when it came to food. I hated eating my meat and vegetables. The more I had to force them down my throat, the more I was turned off and rejected them. It's interesting, though, that as adults, we are more likely to accept (or at least tolerate) whatever is dished up to us in the way of food. We often eventually learn to enjoy the food we once rejected.

I am very much aware that many of the older folk in our churches have to be graciously tolerant regarding the music we utilise in many churches these days. There is a tendency to cater to the tastes of the youth rather than the oldies, although in some churches, it is the other way around. Perhaps it may be helpful for us oldies to bear in mind that our youth are at that crucial stage in their lives where they may well choose to reject anything that is 'put on their plate', so to speak, that is not appealing to them.

I am very blessed to have seen both my children become very much involved in the music in church. I am sure that their enjoyment of the more modern style of worship has contributed to helping them feel connected with the church.

It would be wonderful to strike a perfect balance for everyone concerning the music we utilise for worship in church. If only every person, young and old in our congregations, were able to accept and enjoy the *old* with the *new*. Unfortunately, we do not live in a perfect world yet.

As we move forward into the future as the body and Bride of Christ, I pray that the Holy Spirit will be guiding each of our thoughts and attitudes when we worship Him in song. May we have open hearts and minds to *all* styles of music, as long as it is glorifying to our God. May we know what it truly means to worship in 'spirit and in truth'.

I'm sure many of us know that *'worship is more than just singing a song,'* to quote a line in a song sung in church. I have better understood what it truly means to worship in spirit and in truth in recent years. To come to that place where I feel as though I am surrounded and engulfed by God's presence, intimately communing with Him; spirit joined to Spirit. What a beautiful place to be in, knowing complete union with our creator God and Heavenly Husband.

I long to see a time when the Bride of Christ is wholly united with Him, that the Church will be impacted by the power of the Holy Spirit in ways that we could never imagine. Through intimate daily worship, we will be as one body with Christ: empowered to fulfil our calling as His ambassadors to further establish God's kingdom here on earth.

… SHARON LONGWORTH

I Must Place the Meat on the Altar

One of my favourite passages in the Bible is Romans 12. It is full of instruction on how we are to live our lives as members of the body of Christ, the Church.

Living Sacrifices

Therefore, I urge you, brothers, in view of God's mercy, to offer your bodies as living sacrifices, holy and pleasing to God – which is your spiritual act of worship. Do not conform any longer to the pattern of this world, but be transformed by the renewing of your mind. Then you will be able to test and approve what God's will is - His good, pleasing and perfect will.

For by the grace given me I say to every one of you: Do not think of yourself more highly than you ought, but rather think of yourself with sober judgement, in accordance with the measure of faith God has given you. Just as each of us has one body with many members, and these members do not all have the same function, so in Christ, we who are many form one body, and each member belongs to all the others. We have different gifts, according to the grace given us. If a man's gift is prophesying, let him use it in proportion to his faith. If it is serving, let him serve; if it is teaching, let him teach; if it is encouraging, let him encourage; if it is contributing to the needs of others, let him give generously; if it is leadership, let him govern diligently; if it is showing mercy, let him do it cheerfully.

Love

Love must be sincere. Hate what is evil; cling to what is good. Be devoted to one another in brotherly love. Honor one another above yourselves. Never be lacking in zeal, but keep your spiritual fervor, serving the Lord. Be joyful in hope, patient in affliction, faithful in prayer. Share with God's people who are in need. Practice hospitality.

Bless those who persecute you; bless and do not curse. Rejoice with those who rejoice; mourn with those who mourn. Live in harmony with one another. Do not be proud, but be willing to associate with people of low position. Do not be conceited.

Do not repay evil for evil. Be careful to do what is right in the eyes of everybody. If it is possible, as far as it depends on you, live at peace with everyone. Do not take revenge, my friends, but leave room for God's wrath, for it is written: "It is mine to avenge; I will repay," says the Lord. On the contrary:

"If your enemy is hungry, feed him; If he is thirsty, give him something to drink; In doing this, you will heap burning coals on his head."

Do not be overcome with evil, but overcome evil with good (Romans 12:1-21 NIV).

This passage reminds us that the Church is made up of many individuals who together form one body in Christ. Only as we surrender our lives to Christ can we truly function and work out our calling in unity as His Body.

As in 1 Corinthians 12, we are reminded that each member of the body has been given unique gifts of grace, freely given by God to His people so that we can help meet the needs of the body. These gifts are distributed only by God's grace, according to the measure or proportion of each one's faith. These include gifts of prophecy, ministry, teaching, encouragement and leadership, just to name a few. We are encouraged to love and honour one another, to share with those in need and serve others by practising hospitality. The list instructs how to live our lives serving the Lord with 'spiritual fervour.'

From a human perspective, I find these instructions to be somewhat daunting. I see areas where I fall short and am reminded again of my spiritually stagnant weakness in the flesh. Paul pre-empted these instructions with some essential advice necessary for me to adhere to so that I am able to live up to the standard set out for me as a follower of Christ.

In the first two verses of Romans chapter 12, the mysterious key is found as to how I can know true intimacy with my Heavenly Husband, Jesus, thereby empowering me to take on His attributes as part of His body. The mysterious key I refer to is that of sacrificial worship.

The key to being like Christ as an active member of His body is to be in Christ, an inherited positioning which I was born into at the time of my new birth. Being spiritually positioned in Christ, I am progressively transformed into His likeness. This transformation takes place as I daily lay down my life to Him in sacrificial worship. My mind is gradually being renewed, and I begin to enter that place where I can know God's will for my life.

Due to my spiritually stagnant way of thinking, I once understood worship to be limited to something that I do, such as singing songs in church. This is definitely an integral part of my worship experience, as has been discussed.

Yet, I have realised that true worship is more a state of *being* rather than something I *do*. It is a sincere and sustained attitude deep down in my spirit of submission and reverence to God, my Heavenly Husband.

Living Sacrifices

> Therefore, I **urge** you, brothers, in view of God's mercy, to **offer your bodies as living sacrifices**, holy and pleasing to God – which is your **spiritual worship**. Do not conform any longer to the pattern of this world, but be transformed by the **renewing of your mind**. Then you will be able to test and approve what God's will is - his good, pleasing and perfect will.
>
> (Romans 12: 1-2 NIV) [Emphasis mine].

Paul's words have a sense of urgency as he implores us to offer our bodies as a living sacrifice, holy and pleasing to God. I must place the 'meat' of my fleshly carnal being on the altar, so to speak. In daily surrender to the power of the Holy Spirit, by submitting and allowing Him to control my life, I enter into true spiritual and sacrificial worship. As my spirit and God's Spirit become one, I know intimacy with my Heavenly Husband. Within this beautiful place of union, I no longer live according to the will of my flesh but according to my Heavenly Husband's will.

True spiritual and sacrificial worship begins with a *choice*. My fleshly carnal being enters into true worship when I choose to relinquish my will to God's will. At this point of choice, God's sovereign will takes over.

Please do not misunderstand. God *is* sovereign over His creation and always will be, yet He has created us with the ability to make choices. His desire is that we would *choose* to love and worship Him, that we would long to be so entirely in union with Him that we become like Him; that is, holy and pleasing to Him.

It is a trait of human beings that we are conformed to and live in agreement with whatever it is we worship. Our morals and values are shaped, and our destiny is influenced by whatever or whoever it is we identify with and spend time with. The people or things we hold onto in life as being of the utmost importance to us is what we ultimately worship, whether we realise it or not. It may be the pursuit of material possessions or any number of self indulgences that take the place of putting God and His ways at the forefront of our lives.

We all must choose who or what it is we worship in this life. Only from a place of sacrificial worship do I identify with and come into agreement with God's sovereign will. I must no longer conform to the standards of this world, but instead deliberately choose to love and serve my Heavenly

Husband, being ever aware of the presence of His Holy Spirit, who is waiting for me to simply yield to His will.

Over the years, I have spent much time trying to *figure out* God's will and plan for my life. I realise now that I cannot know God's will through my own intellect or fleshly efforts. Only as I remain in complete union with Christ can I *know* His perfect will.

> ...for it is God who works in you both to **will** and to **do** for His good pleasure (Philippians 2:13 NKJV). [Emphasis mine].

Access into the Holy of Holies through Sacrifice

In the Old Testament, the High Priest was the only person among all the priests permitted to enter into God's presence. He was required to offer up to God a sacrifice of a perfect lamb for the atonement of sins. He would enter through the curtain that hung in the temple, giving him access to the Holy of Holies, the inner tabernacle where God chose to dwell.

This portrays for us a prophetic picture pointing toward Jesus. It is a little tricky to get one's head around this truth as substantiated in God's Word, but Jesus Himself is the fulfilment of every element portrayed in this prophetic picture. Not only is He God's High Priest, but He is also the perfect Sacrificial Lamb that was offered for the atonement of sins. Jesus Himself is, in fact, the Tabernacle. He is the house where God Himself dwells.

At the very moment that Jesus died on the cross, the veil in the temple that separated all but the High Priest from entering into God's presence was torn in two from top to bottom. It was rent at the time of Jesus' crucifixion to show that all men could now come into the presence of God. When Jesus was executed on the cross as the perfect lamb, He provided the way for you and me to enter into God's presence. Through my *faith* in His death and resurrection, I am united with Christ through His Holy Spirit and am permitted to dwell in the very presence of God. In sacrificial worship, as I surrender my life to God, I can know Him intimately.

It is apparent that where there is sacrifice, there must first be surrender. A life must be laid down. Something of value must be given up. Jesus, the living Word and the creator of the universe, surrendered and gave up His life for me. In sacrificial worship, I choose to surrender my life to Him.

In worship, I lay myself on the altar. I give thanks to God for all that He has done. I praise His Holy name as I set my mind on His nature and His all-surpassing goodness. In worship, I become a living sacrifice in response to all that God has done and is. In this place of sacrificial worship, as I submit and become subject to God's will instead of my own will, I become one spirit with my Heavenly Husband. In this beautiful place of sacrificial worship, I find complete intimacy with my God as I enter into His Holy presence. When it comes to sacrificial worship, **'I' am the sacrifice.**

> But the hour is coming, and now is, when the true worshipers will worship the Father in spirit and truth; for the Father is seeking such to worship Him. God is Spirit, and those who worship Him must worship in spirit and truth" (John 4:23-24 NKJV).

Well, I don't know about you, but I am craving a good serving of fruit and vegetables to add to my 'spiritual menu!'

CHAPTER 11

Anyone for Vegetable

As a child, I had a major dislike for vegetables. I suspect I am not alone here. My parents would do their best to persuade me to eat them, usually with the well-used threat that there will be no ice-cream until I eat all my peas! Sound familiar? I would have quite happily lived on bread and butter and Vegemite for the rest of my life. But apparently, as my parents reminded me often, vegetables are good for me. So I would resort to grimacing and forcing them down my throat due to my dire fear of missing out on my much-loved ice-cream. I have since acquired a taste for vegetables. In fact, if I go without my vegies for more than a few days, I begin to crave them.

Speaking of which, may I continue to equate my diet and my craving for vegies with my spiritual walk? I constantly hunger for more of what the Lord has on offer for me as His child. Just as my parents knew what was good for me in vegetables, my Heavenly Father has lots of 'spiritual vegies' that can benefit me as His child.

I have been a member of the Baptist denomination and local church for many years, where I have fed on sound Bible-based teaching. I have *'tasted for myself that the Lord is good* (Psalm 34:8).' My appetite for more of Him continues to increase, causing me to look beyond the walls of the Baptist Church's traditional teaching in the hope of finding more 'vegetables' to satisfy my cravings.

It has been apparent that there are differing opinions within various church denominations concerning the Holy Spirit, or more specifically, the *baptism* of the Holy Spirit. This intrigued me. I had my suspicions that a better understanding of the work of the Holy Spirit may help to satisfy my cravings for 'more' concerning my relationship with God.

As a Baptist, I have always believed that I was born again and *filled* with the Holy Spirit when I accepted Christ as my saviour. On the other hand, your good Pentecostal or Charismatic believes that one is not born again until one is *baptised* with the Holy Spirit and speaks in tongues. I have to say, this confused me.

I understood that the Holy Spirit was poured out on all believers on the Day of Pentecost. Subsequently, since Pentecost, all who believe in the death and resurrection of Jesus receive the filling of the Holy Spirit, and He becomes the seal of their salvation. I never really considered that there may be a difference between being *filled with* and *baptised in* the Holy Spirit. I didn't differentiate between the two.

I now have a slightly different understanding, possibly to the horror of some of my good fellow Baptists. It would seem that the opinions of your typical Baptist and your typical Pentecostal or Charismatic described above are both partly right and partly wrong. To clarify, I still believe that I was filled with the Holy Spirit when I first believed in Jesus' death and resurrection. I know that I was saved and born again into God's family at my conversion to the faith.

Having said that, as I have stressed numerous times, I think there is more to being a born again Christian than I have experienced in the past. I have begun to believe that there is more to be learned and understood concerning the baptism of the Holy Spirit.

The teachings of Derek Prince gave me more clarity in my own understanding of the difference between Baptist teaching and that of Charismatic or Pentecostal teaching on the Holy Spirit. For many years I neglected to notice what took place in John 20:19-22:

> On the evening of that day of the week, when the disciples were together, with the doors locked for fear of the Jews, Jesus came and stood among them and said, "Peace be with you!" After

he said this, he showed them his hands and side. The disciples were overjoyed when they saw the Lord.

Again Jesus said, "Peace be with you! As the Father has sent me, I am sending you." And with that **he breathed on them** and said, **"Receive the Holy Spirit."** (NIV) [Emphasis mine]

I must say, I am shocked that this verse had not been brought to my attention sooner. Its significance is the most crucial and pivotal turning point in the working out of God's purpose of redemption.

So what actually happened at that dramatic moment? Jesus had appeared to His disciples for the first time after His resurrection. It was at this point that the disciples first recognised Him as the risen Christ. At that moment, when they confessed Jesus as their Lord and believed that God had raised Him from the dead, they were saved from eternal condemnation and entered into New Testament salvation. In Romans 10:9, Paul laid down the basic requirements for salvation.

> ...that if you confess with your mouth the Lord Jesus and believe in your heart that God raised Him from the dead, you will be saved.

The inbreathed breath of Jesus imparted to the disciples' new spiritual life. They were born again. Jesus' life giving breath of the Holy Spirit gave them a new identity and authority to do God's will on earth. They were saved from eternal condemnation due to sin. However, it is important to understand that even after this Easter Sunday experience, the total fulfilment of the Holy Spirit had not yet come. After the resurrection, Jesus said the following to His disciples in Luke 24:49:

> "Behold, I send the Promise of My Father upon you; but tarry in Jerusalem until you are endued with power from on high."
> (NKJV)

Shortly after His ascension into heaven, nearly forty days after resurrection Sunday, Jesus said to His disciples:

> "...for John truly baptized with water, but you shall be baptized with the Holy Spirit not many days from now" (Acts 1:5 NKJV).

We see here that resurrection Sunday was not the total fulfilment of the promised Holy Spirit. The complete fulfilment occurred on the Day of Pentecost, which is described in Acts 2:1-4:

When the Day of Pentecost came, they were all together in one place. Suddenly, a sound like the blowing of a violent wind came from heaven and filled the whole house where they were sitting. They saw what seemed to be tongues of fire that separated and came to rest on each of them. All of them were filled with the Holy Spirit and began to speak in other tongues as the Spirit enabled them. (NIV)

We are confronted with two dramatic and wonderful Sundays. The first is Easter Sunday, where we have the resurrected Christ and the inbreathed Spirit. The second is Pentecost Sunday, where we have the glorified Christ and the outpoured Spirit. Each is a pattern for all believers, even today.

Easter Sunday -------->	The Resurrected Christ	The Inbreathed Spirit	Resulting in New Life
Pentecost Sunday -------->	The Glorified Christ	The Outpoured Spirit	Resulting in New Power

I am now more satisfied in my understanding of the difference between being 'filled with' the Spirit and 'baptised in' the Spirit. At my conversion, I was *filled* with the Holy Spirit by the *in-breathed* breath of God. This inbreathed breath caused me to become a new creation in Christ. I was given a new life, having been born again by the Spirit of God. This in-breathed filling of the Holy Spirit will never leave me.

On the other hand, the *baptism* of the Holy Spirit refers to the outpouring of the Holy Spirit, as opposed to the in-breathed. Baptism is usually indicative of one being fully immersed, as in water baptism. Though the infilling of the Holy Spirit at conversion remains, God, in His Sovereignty, administers His out-poured Spirit in varying dimensions and measures as He so pleases. The Pentecost experience of the Holy Spirit is manifested in supernatural 'gifts of power'. God administers these gifts of power to His children as He sees fit, according to His will and purposes, and also according to our measure of faith.

I believe that the Lord longs to bless His children with spiritual vegies. I am referring here to these supernatural gifts of power, otherwise known as 'gifts of the Spirit' or 'spiritual gifts'. God chooses to grant such gifts to better equip His Church for life and ministry, empowering His Bride through the work of the Holy Spirit to represent and partner with Jesus to further establish His kingdom.

I do not wish to portray any negativity toward the Baptist denomination because, for the most part, I am who I am as a Christian due to my Baptist background. However, I feel sad to think that many of my fellow Baptists, and others with conservative evangelical views, may remain ignorant concerning the gifts of the spirit, primarily due to a lack of teaching or understanding of such; some even believing spiritual gifts are not relevant to this day and age.

Opinions and interpretations of scripture vary within any denomination. Yet, we all need to form our own conclusion when it comes to biblical truth.

The Apostle Paul addressed this topic of spiritual gifts in his first letter to the church in Corinth:

> Now concerning spiritual gifts, brethren. **I do not want you to be ignorant**: You know that you are Gentiles, carried away to these dumb idols, however you were led. Therefore I make known to you that no one speaking by the Spirit of God calls Jesus accursed, and no one can say that Jesus is Lord except by the Holy Spirit.
>
> There are diversities of gifts, but the same Spirit. There are differences of ministries, but the same Lord. And there are diversities of activities, but it is the same God who works in all. But the manifestation of the Spirit is given to each one for the profit of all; for to one is given the word of wisdom through

the Spirit, to another the word of knowledge through the same Spirit, to another faith by the same Spirit, to another gifts of healings by the same Spirit, to another the working of miracles, to another prophecy, to another discerning of spirits, to another different kinds of tongues, to another the interpretation of tongues. But one and the same Spirit works all these things, distributing to each one individually as He wills (1 Corinthians 12:1-11 NKJV). [Emphasis mine].

When Paul said, *'Now concerning spiritual gifts, brethren, I do not want you to be ignorant,'* (1 Corinthians 12:1), surely his concerns would apply to the latter-day Church, just as much as they did to the early Church.

I understand that many Christians believe that the gifts are of secondary importance to other aspects of our faith. The emphasis in conservative teaching seems to be on our need to 'strive' to be more like Christ: showing love to our fellow Christians and those around us, and sharing the good news of the Gospel to the unsaved world. Of course, all of these aspects of our faith are of utmost importance and are at the very heart of what we believe as Christians. I most certainly am not refuting this.

However, in ignoring the teaching in God's Word concerning spiritual gifts, we may well be forfeiting the full extent of the blessings and empowerment that I believe God intended for us as His children. Dare I even suggest that God may even be holding back in granting such gifts due to our ignorance and unbelief?

God's purpose in granting spiritual gifts is to encourage and edify His Church, empowering and equipping her through supernatural manifestations of Himself both in and through us, His Bride.

In these latter-days of the Church age, I believe the Lord will use (and is using) supernatural gifts to bring revival and accelerate the establishment of His kingdom; also to *lead* and *protect* His Bride through the tribulations to come.

In Acts chapter 11, we are given an example of how the gift of prophecy is used to provide for the needs of the early Church.

> And in these days prophets came from Jerusalem to Antioch. Then one of them, named Agabus, stood up and showed by the Spirit that there was going to be a great famine throughout all the world, which also happened in the days of Claudius Caesar. Then the disciples, each according to his ability, determined to send relief to the brethren dwelling in Judea. This they also did, and sent it to the elders by the hands of Barnabas and Saul (Acts 11:27-30 NKJV).

In this instance, Agabus prophesied to the believers in Antioch, having been shown by the Holy Spirit through a word of wisdom that a great famine was coming. He was able to warn the disciples, who were then able to act accordingly by sending relief to the Church in Judea. Such prophetic intervention and provision for the saints is already happening within the broader Church and will become more prevalent as we draw closer to the end of the age.

Paul, when instructing the Corinthians to use their gifts in an orderly manner in 1 Corinthians 14:31, said:

> For you can all prophesy one by one, that all may learn and all may be encouraged. (NKJV)

Though we may not hear it spoken of very often in some church circles, or referred to as such, the gift of prophecy is still necessary for kingdom purpose and growth in this day and age. New Testament prophecy could be defined as simply speaking God's will into a situation, declaring what we hear God saying to us through His Spirit to teach, encourage and edify one another. According to the above passage of scripture, it should be a regular part of our lives as Christians.

This is not to say that all prophecy is esteemed to be as equal with God's prophetic Word in scripture. God's written Word is entirely and absolutely authoritative and is not to be judged by man. On the contrary, the gift of prophecy that Paul speaks of in 1 Corinthians 14 must be discerned and judged by others as to its validity and source. Verse 29 says:

Let two or three prophets speak and the others judge.

Verses 32 and 33 say:

And the spirits of the prophets are subject to the prophets. For God is not the author of confusion but of peace, as in all the churches of the saints. (NKJV)

Some believe that the gifts of the Spirit were exclusively appointed to the twelve Apostles when Jesus was on the earth, purely to establish the new Church. I am not aware of anywhere in the Bible that says that the gifts were to cease after a specific time had elapsed. Nor that they were granted exclusively to the twelve Apostles, even though it was to them that He first appointed the gifts. It is, after all, still God's intent and purpose to grow His Church and further establish His kingdom here on earth. Scripture clearly speaks of other disciples in the early Church, besides the twelve, who also actively performed signs and wonders.

Just before His ascent to heaven, Jesus commissioned His followers in Mark 16:15-18 to:

> … "Go into all the world and preach the gospel to every creature. He who believes and is baptized will be saved, but he who does not believe will be condemned. **And these signs will follow those who believe**: In My name they will cast out demons; they will speak with new tongues; they will take up serpents; and if they drink anything deadly, it will by no means hurt them; they will lay hands on the sick, and they will recover."
> (NKJV) [Emphasis mine].

I certainly am not suggesting that we should pick up serpents and drink poison to see what happens. *'You shall not tempt the Lord your God'* (Matthew 4:7) is applicable here, I would suggest. More to my point and emphasis, however, is that Jesus did say that the *supernatural signs and wonders* would follow *those who believe* the teaching of the disciples.

Paul goes on to say that we are all members of one body. Each individual member and their appointed spiritual gifts are necessary for the Church to function effectively. I wonder, are we functioning to our full potential as the body and Bride of Christ? Are we fully yielding to His Spirit, desiring to be used by God through the gifts of His Spirit for the purpose of building His kingdom?

Jesus also said in John 14:12:

> "Most assuredly, I say to you, **he who believes in Me**, the works that I do **he will do also**; and **greater works** than these he will do, because I go to My Father." (NKJV) [Emphasis mine].

Unbelieving Believers

I have heard various reasons and excuses from my fellow believers as to why we should not pursue spiritual gifts in this day and age, none of them standing up very well in my view, I'm afraid to say. One of these reasons being that we may well open ourselves up to the deception of Satan, for he, too, is skilled in the manifestation of supernatural activity.

I acknowledge that Satan is the father of all lies and that it is his business to deceive all who may be susceptible to his ploys. Absolutely, we need to exercise and pray for discernment in this area. We do well to remember that as God's children, Jesus has given us all we need to defeat Satan, having given us complete authority over him by simply claiming the blood of Jesus and declaring His name and His Word as our defence. Are we really going to allow a fear of Satan's deception to keep us from all God would have us be as His Bride and commissioned us to do as disciples of Jesus?

Some believe that if we display the fruits of the Spirit, we do not need to pursue the *gifts* of the Spirit. Yet, the Apostle Paul urges the early Church in 1 Corinthians 12:31:

> But earnestly desire the best gifts. And yet I show you a more excellent way.

Paul then goes on to say in 1 Corinthians 13:1:

> Though I speak with the tongues of men and of angels, **but have not love**, I have become sounding brass or a clanging cymbal. (NKJV) [Emphasis mine].

This verse has been used to support the conviction of some *not* to pursue spiritual gifts. Showing love to others is paramount for Christians. However, do we misunderstand the entirety of what Paul is saying here, taking his words a little out of context? Is Paul really throwing the baby out with the bathwater, so to speak? Is he really saying that our priority as Christians to show love to others should be at the total exclusion and expense of exercising spiritual gifts?

I believe Paul's intent was that exercising spiritual gifts and showing love to others go hand in hand. In verse one of Chapter 14, Paul says, *'Pursue love,* and *desire spiritual gifts, but especially that you may prophesy.'* (NKJV) [Emphasis mine]. The purpose of exercising both love and gifts, apart from glorifying God which goes without saying, is to edify and build up and grow the Church.

Spiritual gifts are of little use in expanding God's kingdom if not exercised and administered with love. Implementing and showing love in our service and ministry to others is essential. The exercising of spiritual gifts, nonetheless, is also beneficial and necessary for God's kingdom purposes. As such, we are told to 'earnestly desire' them.

A Believing Believer - Fearing Failure

You will note that I have been declaring with confidence my belief in God's Word concerning the gifts of the Spirit and their relevance even today. However, I profess to have had minimal experience of such gifting in my own life compared to the testimonies of others.

As keen as I am for God's will and purposes to be done in the granting of spiritual gifts to His Bride, part of me is a little apprehensive about the prospect that such supernatural gifting will become, and already is, a *normal* function in many churches around the world. Would I be correct in suspecting that there may be others who feel the same way?

Are we afraid that with such gifting comes responsibility? Are we afraid that God may require more of us than what we think we are capable of or are comfortable with? Are we worried that we may end up looking foolish?

I comfort myself with the assurance that God is in control. He will be gentle with me, knowing full well my fears, strengths and weaknesses. He will stretch me only according to my faith and according to His empowering.

Ultimately, it is the Lord Himself who is the giver and distributor of His gifts as He so wills and according to our faith. Paul found it necessary to instruct the Corinthians to earnestly desire spiritual gifts. Apparently, they were ignorant as to how the gifts should be operating within the Church. I cannot help but wonder whether this is typical of the latter-day Bride. Could it be that God is waiting for us to *desire* and even *hunger after* His gifts as we approach the end of this age?

I'm sure that many of us would agree that God *is* still granting gifts of prophecy, miracles, tongues and healings and so on, even today. But unfortunately, such amazing signs and wonders do not make headline news for the world to see. Satan makes a point of keeping manifestations of God's power out of the mainstream media, no doubt.

I do not wish to give the impression that I am overly obsessed with my promotion of and desiring after spiritual 'vegies'. But just as my parents knew what was good for me as a child concerning the inclusion of vegies in my diet for my own well being, God is in charge of my spiritual well-being. I trust that He will oversee my spiritual dietary needs.

Whether or not we are unbelieving believers (i.e. believers in Christ, yet not believing that the gifts of the Spirit are for the Church today), there is no denying that people's lives throughout the world are being miraculously transformed due to supernatural manifestations of God's power. My brother-in-law, in fact, was miraculously healed of terminal cancer several years ago. I have included his testimony in a later chapter.

Another Dream

The Lord spoke to me in another dream when I was in the process of writing this chapter. It went like this:

I was at a bible study meeting at the home of our friends. John and Julie (not their real names) *had purchased some vegetables for themselves to eat. John handed me the vegetables he had bought so I could work out what they cost by weighing them.* (A little odd, I know.) *I weighed them on a set of scales that Julie had given me so that I could figure out their worth or value. It was quite an intense process, weighing all these vegetables and coming up with the correct evaluation.*

I woke briefly, contemplating the significance of this dream, and then I drifted again into sleep. The Lord spoke to me again in another dream. (Before I continue, I firstly need to mention that my cousin had popped into my house the previous day. She had given me a block of chocolate to pass on to my sister for her birthday. This seemingly irrelevant information is relevant to my next dream.) It went like this:

I found myself taking the cellophane wrapper off the gift of chocolate my cousin had given me to pass on to my sister. As I removed the outer packaging, I said to myself, 'I shouldn't be taking this off because it's not mine.'

At that point, I woke up. The Holy Spirit spoke to me immediately and said, '*It's not yours to unwrap*'!

Hmmm ... In this chapter, I have been openly expressing my thoughts and opinions concerning the gifts of the Spirit, or spiritual vegies (if you will continue to indulge me in my possibly annoying analogy). According to my first dream, it would seem I have been guilty of *weighing up* the *value* of such 'spiritual vegies' on behalf of my readers, just as I did for my friends in my dream.

The Lord made it quite clear to me in my second dream, however, that it is not my place to *unwrap* the gifts of the Spirit for anybody else. It's up to my readers to *unwrap and weigh up* for themselves the *value* of such gifts. My fear has been that many 'believers' turn up their noses and reject such spiritual vegies, just as I did as a child when it came to eating my vegetables.

We all have differing appetites both in the natural and the spiritual realm. Some are satisfied with the milk of our traditional teachings. Sadly, it seems that we may sometimes prefer to *substitute* spiritual *vegies* with spiritual *Vegemite*, choosing not to be too adventurous when it comes to tasting all that God is offering to His children in the way of spiritual vegies. Little do we realise the blessings and the spiritual ice-cream we may be missing out on, possibly due to ignorance or unbelief. When we hunger after all that God has purposed for His children, He is faithful in availing to us treasures we never thought were possible for us to possess.

All this to say that I desire to *put my hand up*, so to speak, to everything God has on offer to me as His child. I am all for bringing on the spiritual vegies if this is God's will for my life.

I am hoping and praying that you, too, may acquire a hunger for more vegies. That is, if you are not already feeling a little peckish!

CHAPTER 12

Top it off with a Feast of Fruit Salad for Dessert

'It must have been one huge and shiny red apple! That's if it was, in actual fact, an apple!' This thought process went through my mind at about three o'clock one morning. I was thinking about the piece of fruit that Adam and Eve ate in the Garden of Eden.

Paradise on earth was lost due to the self-indulgent cravings of Adam and Eve over what must have been a deliciously good-looking piece of fruit. It was over a piece of fruit that the world is now steeped in corruption, taking on qualities that are ironically somewhat similar to that of the degenerating process of a rotten apple. Once a tiny spot of rot sets in, there is no turning back the corrosion process. Eventually, the whole apple becomes totally decayed, and so it is with our degenerating world.

As I was thinking about these things, it occurred to me that another type of fruit is instrumental in restoring Paradise on earth. Only as I appropriate this type of fruit into my spiritual menu will 'fruit' be the bearer of *life* to humanity again instead of *death*. As I am grafted into the life-giving vine who is Jesus and abide there with Him, good fruit will be produced in my life. Jesus said:

> I am the vine, you are the branches. He who abides in Me, and I in him, bears much fruit; for without Me you can do nothing (John 15:5 NKJV).

The fruits of the Spirit are love, joy, peace, patience, kindness, goodness, faithfulness, gentleness and self-control. As my life produces and cultivates these fruits, I will once again begin to reflect God's likeness.

Not only should my life produce *good* fruit, but I need to produce *seed-bearing* fruit. As new seeds are planted and propagated into the lives of others, the Holy Spirit does His work of fertilising them with life-giving water. These newly birthed seeds will produce more branches, thereby adding further growth to God's kingdom in preparation for the final harvest.

God the Father, the vine-dresser, lovingly tends to the vine by pruning the branches. He prunes every branch that bears good fruit so that it may reproduce more fruit. The scary part is that every branch that does not bear fruit is cut away and thrown into the fire. The pruning process can be painful, but ultimately it causes me to flourish, cultivating an eventual harvest of fruit that brings glory and honour to my Heavenly Father.

By this My Father is glorified, that you bear much fruit; so you will be My disciples (John 15:8 NKJV).

Psalm 1:1-3 is one of my favourite passages that I love to 'speak out loud' regularly. It paints a beautiful picture of how seasonal fruit is produced in our lives as we delight in and meditate daily on God's Word.

Blessed is the man Who walks not in the counsel of the ungodly, Nor stands in the path of sinners, Nor sits in the seat of the scornful; But his **delight** is in the law of the Lord, and in His law he **meditates** day and night. He shall be like a tree Planted by the rivers of water, That **brings forth its fruit in its season**, Whose leaf also shall **not wither**: And whatever he does shall **prosper**. (NKJV) [Emphasis mine].

What a beautiful incentive to stay intimately connected to the vine who is Jesus, and to remain planted by the rivers of water, receiving daily nourishment through God's Word. Only as I abide in Christ can I bear the fruits of His Spirit, which gradually manifest in my life to reflect the nature of Jesus.

Imagine if every believer were shining lights displaying for the world to see the fruits of love, joy, peace, patience, kindness, goodness, faithfulness, gentleness and self-control. Such fruits would go a long way toward regenerating our sad and fallen world.

Through various dreams, visions and impressions, the Lord has given me a *spiritual menu* of bread and butter and meat and vegies to supplement the 'milk' that I had survived on for many years in my spiritual journey. In my hunger for more of Him, the Lord has patiently and graciously allowed me to taste and see that He is good. I continue to discover that there is so much more to enjoy and savour as a Christian beyond drinking milk. All I need now is a good serving of healthy fruit salad to complete my meal.

My Spiritual Menu to Combat Spiritual Stagnation

Milk - Living according to the flesh (from which I am slowly but surely being weaned). For many years, I was feeding only on milk, inhibiting my spiritual growth. I lived reliant on the strength of my fleshly carnal nature instead of relying on the power of the Holy Spirit who is in me. To mature as a Christian, I must add more 'solid food' to my spiritual diet.

Butter - The 'mindset' that kept me enslaved to the power of the flesh.

As I began to grow in my walk with the Lord, I was feeding well on the elementary truths of God's Word, yet I was still hungry and craving for more. I discovered that 'butter', representing my slave-to-the-flesh mentality, is transformed and becomes satisfying and *empowering* when applied to the Bread of life, who is Jesus.

Bread - Jesus the Bread of life.

It is only in Jesus, the Bread of Life, that I find my daily source of empowerment. Knowing my true identity as a new creation 'in Christ', I am empowered to overcome my spiritually stagnant battle with my fleshly carnal nature. As a Christian, the key to empowerment is not through effort but through intimate union with Jesus, the Bread of life.

Meat - Sacrificial worship

I am learning to lay my life down as a living sacrifice in daily submission to my Heavenly Husband, allowing Him to take complete control of all that I am and do. Then I begin to live my life according to His will. I cultivate an *intimate union* with Him as I bask in His presence in sacrificial worship. I begin to understand what it truly means to worship in spirit and truth daily, minute-by-minute.

Vegetables - Gifts of the Spirit

God is able to manifest Himself through me by His Spirit. As my spiritual appetite and faith increase and God so wills, the Holy Spirit adds a side dish of vegies to my menu. He begins to reveal Himself through dreams and visions, and I gradually learn to recognise His voice. He begins to endow me with *spiritual gifts of power* for the further edification of His Bride and ultimately for His own glorification.

Fruit - Fruits of the Spirit

As I remain grafted to the vine who is Jesus, He begins to produce beautiful fruits of the Spirit in me: *love, joy, peace, patience, kindness, goodness, faithfulness, gentleness and self-control.* The fruits of His nature are gradually cultivated in my life. Then as I ripen and mature, more seeds are able to be produced and propagated, causing increase and growth in the expansion of His kingdom, bringing glory and honour to my Heavenly Father.

PART V

Spiritual Gifts

CHAPTER 13

The Gift of Tongues

In chapter six, I wrote of my desperation for assurance that I did, in actual fact, have the Holy Spirit living in me. I prayed that the Lord would grant me the gift of speaking in tongues as proof of His abiding presence. That same night, I experienced a dream and a vision from the Lord. I had a genuine sense of the Lord telling me that the gift of speaking in tongues was not the only indication that one had the Holy Spirit living inside.

He told me that the gift of prophecy is also an indication of the indwelling Holy Spirit and is even more desirable and beneficial than the gift of tongues, because the gift of prophecy is helpful to build up and edify the Church. On the other hand, the gift of tongues is generally only edifying to the recipient of that gift unless it is followed by an interpretation for the benefit of the Church.

All that the Lord had revealed to me in the early hours of the morning was confirmed to me later that day when I sought God's Word for confirmation of what He had impressed upon me.

> Pursue love, and desire spiritual gifts, but especially that you may prophesy. For he who speaks in a tongue does not speak to men but to God, for no one understands him; however, in the spirit he speaks mysteries. But he who prophesies speaks edification and exhortation and comfort to men. He who speaks in a tongue edifies himself, but he who prophesies edifies the church. I wish you all spoke with tongues, but even more that you prophesied; for he who prophesies is greater than he who speaks with tongues, unless indeed he interprets, that the church may receive edification (1 Corinthians 14:1-5 NKJV).

I accepted, at that time, that I did not receive the gift of tongues as I had requested. I was open to God's will, and it would seem that He had more important things to teach me.

As it turned out, what seemed to be a 'no' from the Lord was actually a 'not just yet.' Three years later, in March of 2012, the Lord graciously chose to grant me the gift of praying in tongues. My Dad was very ill in Royal North Shore hospital in Sydney at the time, having undergone five lots of surgery over three weeks. He was hospitalised in Sydney for six weeks, then back in Taree for another couple of months.

THE GIFT OF TONGUES

My mum and my sister Janine stayed with him in Sydney the whole time. Janine had taken long service leave from her job to be able to do so. I needed to continue working, so I drove down to Sydney every weekend to see them. On one of these trips, I was listening to a teaching CD of Derek Prince on the subject of spiritual gifts and the baptism of the Holy Spirit.

Though my initial prayer request of speaking in tongues had seemingly been denied by the Lord, I continued to have a yearning to experience this gift if the Lord was so willing. To be granted such a gift from God would be an assurance for me of the presence of His Holy Spirit indwelling my being.

As I was driving along and listening to Derek Prince teaching on the baptism of the Spirit, He gave instruction on how to receive the gift of tongues, followed by a prayer.

I sense there may be some who, in reading this, may have suddenly felt somewhat indignant, feeling a degree of scepticism concerning what I just said. You may be asking yourself, 'How can anyone give instruction on how to receive the gift of tongues? The gift of tongues can only be given by the will and sovereignty of God. Nobody can initiate the giving or the receiving of something that is only God's to give.'

You are right! I totally agree. But this is the way it happened for me. I understand that thousands of others have come under this instruction and have freely received the baptism. Only God knows the hearts of those who come under such instruction. Only He will be the judge as to whom He decides will receive His grace in granting His spiritual gifts.

As I was driving down the highway, I felt a sense of anticipation deep within as I repeated after Derek a prayer that went like this:

> *Lord Jesus Christ, I believe that You are the Son of God and that on the cross You died for my sins and rose again from the dead. I trust you for forgiveness and for cleansing. I believe You received me as a child of God. And because You have received me, I receive myself as a child of God.*
>
> *If there's any resentment in my heart now, any unforgiveness against anyone, I lay it down. I forgive every other person as I would have God forgive me. If I've ever been involved in the occult, I acknowledge that as a sin. I ask Your forgiveness and I loose myself now from every contact with Satan and with occult power in the name of Jesus.*
>
> *And now, Lord Jesus, I come to You as my Baptiser in the Holy Spirit. I present to You my body to be a temple of Your Spirit. I yield to You my tongue to be an instrument of righteousness, to worship You in a*

new language. By faith, I receive this now, and I thank You for it in the name of Jesus.

Amen.

As I was praying this prayer, I began to feel the Holy Spirit welling up inside me. I experienced a sense of stirring deep down in my belly. I simply breathed in, opened my mouth, and began to speak an unknown language, articulating and forming the words 'as the Spirit gave me utterance'.

> And they were all filled with the Holy Spirit and began to speak with other tongues, as the Spirit gave them utterance (Acts 2:4 NKJV).

Out of my mouth came a beautiful prayer language, a little tentatively at first, but soon began to flow fluently through my lips. This prayer language is sometimes known as the heavenly language. What a blessing it was to receive such a beautiful gift, having just passed through the town of Bulahdelah and heading south down the highway. I spent the rest of the trip to Sydney communing with the Lord, His Holy Spirit speaking through me.

I suspect the Lord chose to give me this gift at that particular time so that His Spirit would intercede through me for my Dad's recovery. Of course, I did not recognise the language I was speaking, yet as I was driving along praying, one word would flow from my mouth with almost every sentence. I recognised this particular word, though it is not one I would normally use myself. It is an affectionate term of endearment used in several languages for 'daddy' or 'father.' The word that I am referring to is 'Papa.'

To have this beautiful word 'Papa' flowing fluently from my mouth was confirmation for me that this was, in actual fact, a genuine unknown language that I was speaking. Was the Holy Spirit praying earnestly for my dear earthly Dad, my Papa? Or was He using the word Papa to address my Heavenly Father? I do not know for sure. I know that it was an incredible comfort to hear this beautiful word of endearment flow frequently from my mouth. My Dad was oh so very ill, and my heart was broken in an earnest plea for his recovery. My own words could not have expressed the depth of need and desire that I felt at the time, wanting so desperately for my Dad to survive. It was such a comfort to know that Jesus Himself was likely pleading to the Father through the Holy Spirit for my Dad's recovery.

Considering all the major surgeries my beautiful Dad endured in such a short period, it is definitely miraculous that he survived. The Lord heard my cries and the cries of the many others who were earnestly praying for him, also.

On the way home from one of my trips to Sydney, as I was praying in my new prayer language, the Lord spoke to me in the gentle whisper of His Spirit. He said, '*You are my child, and I love you. All will be well with your Dad. He will rise up and walk.*'

We were so very grateful to the Lord that Dad did rise up and walk again. Weak and crippled as he was, Dad attended Nimali and Matthew's wedding the following November, although he was not very well at the time. Dad passed away approximately six weeks later at 1a.m. on the 1st of January, 2013. Had it been 'eastern standard time' instead of 'daylight savings time', he would have passed away right on the dot of midnight, being right at the end of one year and the very beginning of another. God was gracious in raising him up for a time, allowing him to be able to attend his granddaughter's wedding and to spend one last Christmas with us all.

◇◇◇◇◇◇◇◇

Dad had suffered terribly for several years due to quite a number of health issues. Yet his faith in God remained strong and sure, as was the case with my mum. The morning that Dad died, the Lord graciously spoke a word of comfort to Mum through His Word. Being the beautiful Christian lady she is, devoted to her Lord in reading His Word daily, she opened her Bible, which just 'happened' to fall open at Psalm 34. We know that the Lord had His finger on the page. I will only note here to verse eight:

> I will bless the Lord at all times; His praise shall continually be in my mouth. My soul shall make its boast in the Lord; The humble shall hear of it and be glad. Oh, magnify the Lord with me, And let us exalt His name together.
>
> **I sought the Lord, and He heard me, And delivered me from all my fears.** They looked to Him and were radiant, And their faces were not ashamed. **This poor man cried out, and the Lord heard him, And saved him out of all his troubles.**
>
> **The angel of the Lord encamps around all those who fear Him, And delivers them. Oh, taste and see that the Lord is good; Blessed is the man who trusts in Him** (Psalm 34:1-8 NKJV)! [Emphasis mine].

The Lord assured Mum, in verse six, that He had heard Dad's cry and had saved him from all his troubles. Verse eight was also significantly meaningful to her. Mum had found a handwritten copy of Dads testimony in the cover of his old Bible, which was falling apart due to much use. (I have included a copy of Dad's testimony at the end of this book). The very last words that Dad had noted in his testimony were found in verse eight of the above passage: **Oh taste and see that the Lord is good; Blessed is the man who trusts in Him.**

What a wonderful, loving and gracious God we serve, who longs to pour out His blessings upon His children. It is such a privilege to experience the comforting voice of the Lord when He speaks to us in our times of need. The more we desire and seek after Him, and attune our ears to His voice, the more He reveals Himself to us.

These past few years have turned out to be a significant turning point in my walk with the Lord. I have continued on in the blessing of my new prayer language. I am finally beginning to experience **'the more'** that I longed for as a Christian. My appetite is definitely increasing for more 'solid food' as I continue to taste and see that the Lord is good!

Even so, I sense this is just the beginning of my journey in growing from **infancy** to **intimacy** with my Lord.

CHAPTER 14

The Gift of Prophecy

My first encounter with a person gifted in the prophetic actually occurred in our local Baptist Church. It was towards the end of a marriage seminar that Andrew and I attended early in our marriage. The visiting speaker announced that he would work his way around the room to those in attendance and prophesy into each person's life.

This was something totally new and foreign to me. He began speaking to those around me with words he believed to be specific messages from God. As he was doing so, I began to squirm a little in my seat. I looked around in the hope of trying to discern what others were feeling concerning this strange turn of events. I had never experienced anything such as this in our conservative Baptist Church before. I suspect that there were probably many other people who were also feeling a little apprehensive, if the truth be known.

I was asking myself, '*Is it possible that this man is actually hearing from God? I mean, is this for real?*' Our church rarely discussed such things as the

THE GIFT OF PROPHECY

baptism of the Holy Spirit, the gifts of tongues and prophecy and the like. It seemed to me that to speak of such things was taboo. At least, that was my perception at the time. I was intrigued as this apparent modern-day prophet went from person to person, speaking into each one's life. I was curious to know just how accurate his words were and whether those receiving them could relate in any way to what he was saying.

And then it was my turn. When I think back, I believe I almost held my breath as he spoke. I was thinking, *'Could this really be God speaking to me through this man?'* He quoted a verse of scripture that he believed the Lord would have me take particular notice to. He seemed a little uncertain as to why the Lord gave me this verse, yet he had his wife write down the reference on a piece of paper, and she handed it to me. I wasn't sure of what the verse meant either, nor how it applied to me. It almost seemed cryptic, in fact. I stored that piece of paper away in the cover of my Bible for future reference.

Several years later, when I decided to revisit its contents, I discovered that the piece of paper had gone astray. I was very disappointed, although I had a feeling that I would recognise the verse if I ever came across it again, because the words of this modern-day prophet had stuck in my mind from that day. He had said to me, *'Take the old with the new!'* This was the message he believed the Lord would have me hold onto from this verse. *'Take the old with the new!'*

Before writing this book, I had the privilege of being in touch with a lovely cousin whom the Lord has endowed with beautiful spiritual gifts. She would often send me words of encouragement via email. In one of these emails, on the web page of a Christian organisation, I spotted a verse of scripture. It was written in such tiny print that I could barely read it. I am convinced that it was the verse given to me as a word of prophecy, or a word of wisdom, many years beforehand. In God's perfect timing, He revealed to me again this verse:

> He said to them, "Therefore every teacher of the law who has been instructed about the kingdom of heaven is like the owner of a house who brings out of his storeroom **new** treasures as well as **old**" (Matthew 13:52 NIV). [Emphasis mine].

Jesus had been speaking to the people in parables. The disciples were questioning Jesus as to why He spoke in mysteries. Parables compel listeners to discover the truth, while at the same time, the truth is concealed from those who are not genuinely open to receiving it. Those who do not wholeheartedly desire to understand the mystery hidden in the words of

Jesus. To those who are honestly searching, the truth becomes clear. Jesus was not hiding the truth from sincere seekers because those receptive to spiritual truth understood the illustrations, or at least they did eventually. In these parables, Jesus was teaching His disciples about the kingdom of heaven.

For many years, my only understanding of the kingdom of heaven was that it is a place in eternity where those who have faith in the saving grace of Jesus will go when we die. My view has not changed significantly, yet there is so much more to be understood concerning God's kingdom. In more recent years, I have more precisely identified the kingdom of heaven as being a spiritual realm where God rules. We share in God's eternal kingdom when we trust in Jesus as our Saviour and allow Him to be Lord and ruler of our lives. Jesus sheds some light on this in Luke 17:20-21:

> Now when He was asked by the Pharisees when the kingdom of God would come, He answered them and said, "The kingdom of God does not come with observation; nor will they say, 'See here!' or 'See there!' For indeed, the kingdom of God is within you." (NKJV)

The kingdom of God and its attributes are part of our everyday life experience through the indwelling Holy Spirit.

> ... for the kingdom of God is not eating and drinking, but righteousness and peace and joy in the Holy Spirit (Romans 14:17 NKJV).

The kingdom of heaven is where God rules. We do not have to wait until we die to experience the wonders, attributes and treasures of the kingdom of heaven whilst ever the Lord is reigning over our lives. As the Bride of Christ, we can have a taste of this spiritual realm in the here and now.

I am discovering *'new treasure'* from the storeroom of God's eternal kingdom that is part of my inheritance as His child. The Lord's Word is a huge treasure box full of secrets and mysteries that He longs to share with His children. I have been grounded in the *old* and steadfast Word of God for many years, yet I know that I have barely touched the surface in my understanding of the mysteries contained in the Bible. I am now becoming much more aware that there are *new* treasures in God's Word to be found.

Way back when the prophetic word was first given to me, being *'take the old with the new'*, the Lord knew where I would be in my spiritual journey at this time of my life, many years later. It was a huge encouragement to come across this verse again when it was particularly relevant to me. A time when I have been discovering and 'weighing up' for myself the truths and promises of God's Word that are 'new' to me, at least.

I had recently enjoyed discussions with my cousin about the incredible ways God had been working in her life. We also spoke about the things the Lord had been teaching me in recent times. We would talk about how God seemingly loves to send His children on a treasure hunt of hide-and-go-seek. He would reveal just enough of Himself to make us hunger for more of Him. I related to this because God had been revealing Himself to me through the mystery of dreams and visions, and through teaching me to be sensitive to His voice and the interpretation of His leading. Due to these things, my belief has been affirmed that the gift of prophecy is still relevant today.

The treasures that Jesus refers to in Matthew 13:52 are the secret mysteries and truths found only in the supernatural spiritual realm of God's kingdom such as God-inspired revelation, wisdom, knowledge and understanding; and God-given righteousness, peace and joy in the Holy Spirit, and so on. The most profound mystery of all is that Christ is *in me*, as referred to in Colossians 1:27. God reveals His secrets and unknown mysteries to those of His children who hunger after them. When we search for His treasures with a sincere heart and motives, God begins to reveal Himself and His kingdom purposes to us as we abide in close union with His Spirit.

Many *new* treasures, gifts, and mysteries of God are yet to be discovered, but I still hold firmly to the *old* foundational truths of God's Word that are at the very heart of my salvation and knowledge of Him. I anticipate 'taking the old *with* the new' and look forward to appropriating into my life the spiritual inheritance that is mine in Christ.

Another Encounter with a Modern-day Prophet

'God wants to impregnate you with His Word!'

These words were spoken by a preacher whose church I had visited for a short period. This was my second visit. I sat in the congregation next to my cousin, about two or three rows back from the front. There were many other people in the room, yet the words of this preacher were spoken directly to me. How do I know this? I know because this man of God had his arm fully outstretched and was pointing his finger straight at me. He was standing only a few paces away, and his eyes were fixed firmly on mine. It seemed as though there was nobody else in the room. I felt a stirring in my belly, sensing God Himself was speaking directly into my life through this man.

On our first visit to this church, the week before this, the same pastor had spoken prophetic words of wisdom into my cousin's life that were very applicable and affirming for her. The presence of the Holy Spirit is evident in this man's life. He hears words of knowledge and wisdom from the Lord and is obedient in speaking such words of encouragement, edification and instruction to the Church, as God so directs.

As he spoke into my life, I was intrigued by his use of the word 'impregnate.' As you know, I have never before conceived a child, as the word impregnate would commonly apply. Perhaps the Lord knew that this word would have a way of impacting my senses, taking hold of my attention. As I considered the use of this word, I was reminded of something I had experienced many years prior. It happened within a few months of having been told that it was most unlikely that Andrew and I would conceive a child. I distinctly remember being in the backyard of our house at Taree West, where we were living at the time. I was at the clothesline pegging out the washing when a still small voice seemingly spoke to me deep down in my spirit. I believed that God told me that I would become pregnant in the latter part of my life. It may well be that the prospect of becoming pregnant was purely wishful thinking. Still, for some reason, this experience has stayed with me.

I wonder whether what I believed to be a word from the Lord back then was relevant to this recent prophetic word spoken over me. In God's mysteriously cryptic way, perhaps He was actually telling me that He desired to impregnate me *with His Word* in these latter-days; as I am maturing both physically and spiritually (His ways and thoughts being different to mine).

It may well be that I am clutching at straws! Whether this be the case or not, God's desire is that my life would be the product of His Word. God's desire is that my life would produce life-giving fruit as I abide in Him and in His Word. God's written Word is, in actual fact, the living Word of Christ Himself. His Word is the fertile ground through which my life would propagate fruits of the Spirit: love, joy, peace, patience, kindness, goodness, faithfulness, gentleness and self-control. When a seed is planted in the fertile ground, it takes root. It receives nourishment from the nutrients it is planted in, causing it to prosper and grow until it eventually bears fruit. It is the same as when a seed is conceived in a woman's womb and is fertilised. It ultimately brings forth new life.

I have often admired people who are so grounded in God's Word that they can quote scripture from memory. Or they know exactly what scripture passage to turn to concerning a particular topic. Over the years, I have managed to memorise many verses of scripture. Yet, I could not retain such verses for any length of time. To my shame, I am very much aware that this was due to my lack of discipline when it came to the in-depth and repetitive study of God's Word.

Ever since I was fifteen years old, I have *devotedly* taken time each day to 'read' my Bible or a devotional of some description. I have been very *sincere* in my desire to increase my knowledge of God through regular Bible reading. But, I have known for some time that I fall a long way short of giving to God all that is desired of me when it comes to spending quality time with Him. I have had good intentions, and my heart longs to spend so much more time with my Lord in prayer and worship and study of His Word than I seem to be able to manage. Yet, life itself would have to come to a complete standstill for me to be able to give back to the Lord all that He is deserving of in my time and devotion, in the physical sense, at least.

Since the Lord spoke to me directly through this preacher, I have become more determined to spend time with God, studying and memorising His Word. I have made *some* progress with managing this area of my life, although I am still very conscious of my shortcomings.

I am aware, though, that sometimes it is easy to simply read a passage of scripture for the sake of reading a passage of scripture, because we know as Christians that this is what we need to do to grow in our faith. Nevertheless, in reading God's Word over the years, I have grown in my faith and knowledge of Him. I am learning to apply and appropriate His teaching into my life.

My heart has always been in the right place, yet I have now discovered something more profound and life-changing as I read my Bible. The scriptures are becoming even more alive to me since I have grown in my understanding and awareness of the Holy Spirit in my life, being more conscious of His presence within me.

> **For the word of the Lord is living and powerful**, and sharper than any two-edged sword, piercing even to the division of soul and spirit, and of joints and marrow, and is a discerner of the thoughts and intents of the heart (Hebrew 4:12 NKJV). [Emphasis mine].

> My son, give attention to my words; Incline your ear to my sayings. Do not let them depart from your eyes; Keep them in the midst of your heart; **For they are life to those who find them,** And health to all their flesh (Proverbs 4:20-22 NKJV). [Emphasis mine].

My faith is fertilised and developed through reading the written Word of God regularly, bringing me closer to maturity in my new life in Christ, although it's not quite that simple. I don't necessarily grow and develop faith by simply 'reading' the Bible.

> So then faith comes by **hearing**, and hearing by the word of God (Romans 10:17 NKJV). [Emphasis mine].

This verse does not say that faith comes by 'reading' the Word of God. I actually have to *hear* the Word of God as I read it for it to impact my life. This is not to say that I must read the words out loud, although, this can be very beneficial and is a practice that is becoming a regular part of my daily routine. The Scriptures are, in fact, God's *spoken* Word. They were put to pen and paper by the scribes and the prophets to whom God spoke through the inspiration of the Holy Spirit to reveal His will and purposes for humanity.

> **All scripture is given by inspiration of God,** and is profitable for doctrine, for reproof, for correction, for instruction in righteousness, that the man of God may be complete, thoroughly equipped for every good work (2 Timothy 3:16-17 NKJV). [Emphasis mine].

God's Word is made alive through the power and inspiration of the Holy Spirit. One does not necessarily acquire faith simply by listening to a preacher or reading the Bible. Faith comes through the active power of the Holy Spirit working through God's spoken Word. Understanding comes, and my faith is developed, as I listen with an open heart - yielded to the Holy Spirit and attuned to God's voice - being ready and willing to hear what He has to say to me.

I was already aware of my shortcomings as far as spending quality time in God's Word was concerned when the prophetic word was spoken over me that night. As I previously mentioned, I had been blessed to be reacquainted with my cousin, with whom I had been quite close in our younger years. Spending time with her made it evident that she was totally in love with and devoted to her Heavenly Husband. She would spend hours reading and studying the scriptures, rising in the very early hours, eager to spend time with her Lord. Her example left me feeling ashamed of my lack of devotion and commitment to spending time with my Heavenly Husband. The Lord knew that I needed a reasonably severe prod to jolt me into action.

I am very grateful that God used this man, whom I believe is gifted in the prophetic, to give me an extra nudge that night. I am the first to admit that I am not very intellectually minded nor gifted in knowledge concerning most things in life. I certainly have no formal training in theology. But thankfully, God does not require that I *be* grounded in *theology*. He longs for me to be grounded *in Him* and in the truths and treasures of His Word. He reveals them to me through the power of His Holy Spirit, granting understanding according to His wisdom, not mine.

CHAPTER 15

The Gift of Healing

I previously mentioned that my brother-in-law was miraculously healed of cancer. Here is his story:

David's Story – Six Weeks to Live

Life has been good for me, dare I say easy, though I don't mind hard work and long hours. God has blessed me in many ways with His guidance and His provision of family, employment, friends and too many coincidences (God-incidences) to count. But I have had a nagging doubt that God does not trust me with hardship.

....

In November 2007, I was in John Hunter Hospital after some exploratory keyhole surgery when the senior surgeon came to me and said, 'I'm sorry to have to tell you this, but you're not going to make it to Christmas.'

My difficulties had started about a month earlier when I discovered I couldn't bend over and pick up the bits of rubbish on the ground. Then over a couple of days, I was having trouble breathing and could only manage to shuffle around. I was admitted to hospital, where they were able to help me breathe by sticking a tube in my side and drain fluid from my lung cavity. My friend, a nurse, said, 'You will experience some slight discomfort'. What an understatement! This was repeated about every five days. I had scans and tests which showed I had a large mass in my abdomen, which was assumed to be pancreatic cancer. The surgery at John Hunter hospital had been to gain better information.

When I was first admitted to Taree hospital, a work colleague sent emails to all the Christian Schools, Churches and Christians who regularly holiday or have camps at Camp Elim, where I am the manager.

Replies started flooding back, telling me of all the people who were praying for me. The Staff at some Christian Schools were praying for me three times a day. One teacher who just loves Camp Elim food sent numerous emails of encouragement. A couple from Ariah Park in western NSW organised with friends in Texas, USA, to pray for me during their waking hours while my friends slept the night away in Australia, which meant I was literally being prayed for twenty-four hours a day. That was incredibly encouraging whilst laying awake at night in hospital listening to a book review on the best way to die and a country and western song about a cowboy whose wife, dog, and horse had left, gone blind, broken a leg and had to be shot.

In Revelation, it talks about the prayers of the saints – (just everyday Christians) being the incense in God's throne room. It is a great comfort when you have been told you only have a few more weeks to live to know so many people are praying for you and that their prayers are a beautiful aroma in God's presence.

The biopsy from the surgery indicated the type of cancer I had (Non Hodgkin's Lymphoma Type B aggressive) and with it a glimmer of hope, as this was the preferable option to pancreatic cancer, and so it was arranged that I would have chemotherapy.

In the time between having the biopsy and starting chemotherapy, a lady from church asked if she and her husband could come and anoint me with oil and pray for me. She had been sensing the prompting of the Lord for a couple of weeks and came to the conclusion that if she did nothing, she would be being disobedient to God. A small group of friends and family gathered in our home, where prayer was offered on my behalf, and I was anointed with oil.

Shortly after this, I was required to have a PET scan. The results of this were 'inconclusive', which was medical terminology for 'confusion' or 'disbelief' because the scan was 'clear' where cancer should have been clearly visible. Our prayers were answered, and I had been miraculously healed. We asked if it was necessary to have the chemotherapy since there was no indication of cancer, but the doctors recommended it – 'just in case'.

I had six doses of chemotherapy over an 18 week period. Each dose was a full-day event of having numerous bags of 'stuff' dripped into my body. I was very fortunate not to have many of the horrendous side effects suffered by some people undergoing chemotherapy. I had a dream run through the 21 weeks though the middle week of each cycle was a bit harrowing. I only made the trip down and up the stairs at home once each day. Trips to do the shopping and errands had to be planned according to the degree of slope of the footpaths I had to walk, though none of them have much of an incline.

My kids both had assurances from God our Father that I wouldn't die. Our daughter was led to a verse which says, 'This illness is not unto death,' which is in the story of Lazarus (John 10:4).

On one of my post-surgery trips to John Hunter Hospital, I heard a surgeon exclaim loudly in the corridor when looking at my latest scans, 'There must be some mistake. These can't possibly be Mr Hayes' scans'.

On another trip back to John Hunter Hospital, a doctor who helped with my care and diagnosis in Taree had by this stage transferred to Newcastle and was now a consultant at John Hunter Hospital. Her jaw nearly hit the floor before a big smile lit up her face when she recognised me and I was obviously alive and well.

About 12 months later, one of my son's mates who works at Taree hospital asked about my health and if I was having any adverse and ongoing problems because, as he said, 'the word around the hospital at the time was that I was stuffed'.

I wasn't concerned for myself about dying, and my wife and I were both at peace in God's assurances of heaven for believers.

How great a heavenly Father we have who knows our hearts and thoughts and gives us the desires of our hearts, even if it means living through an illness.

◇◇◇◇◇◇◇◇

I remember well the night I received the dreaded phone call from my sister, Janine. She was phoning from Newcastle, having just been told that David probably would not see Christmas. Christmas was only six weeks away! How could this possibly be?

I cannot describe the sense of disbelief and dread I felt as she relayed to me the news that nobody ever wants to hear. I immediately wanted to jump in the car and drive to Newcastle to be with my big sister as she was alone at the time, David being in hospital. I must say, in light of the devastating news she had just received, I was amazed at the calmness in her voice as she spoke. She assured me that she would be fine, and as it turned out, she was.

David mentioned in his testimony, and Janine later testified that they both experienced a somewhat surreal peace, even though the bottom had just fallen out of their world. This peace could only have come from the Lord.

The night I received the devastating news from Janine, I came before the Lord and prayed as I had never prayed before in my life. God's throne room must have been so abundantly high with the aroma of incense due to the prayers of David's many family members and friends pleading for David's healing and deliverance from this insidious disease. All praise and glory to God who heard our prayers and chose to intervene with His hand of healing.

I sincerely believe that God initiated David's healing through the actions of the lady from church, whose husband was one of our Pastors. Having been prompted by the Holy Spirit to do so, she organised for a small group of family and friends to anoint David with oil and lay hands on him in prayer. I am convinced that her obedience to the Lord's prompting was instrumental in the healing taking place.

We are told in James 5:14-16:

> Is any one of you sick? He should call the elders of the church to pray over him and anoint him with oil in the name of the Lord. And the prayer offered in faith will make the sick person well; the Lord will raise him up. If he has sinned, he will be

forgiven. Therefore confess your sins to each other and pray for each other so that you may be healed. The prayer of a righteous man is powerful and effective. (NIV)

I am so grateful that the Lord heeded the cry of His saints and that He rewarded the actions of this special lady. She was prepared to move out of her comfort zone in obedience to God's instruction, initiating the anointing of David with oil and the laying on of hands in prayer.

I often look at David in absolute wonder and awe, feeling an overwhelming sense of gratitude for God's goodness and grace. To think that David is still with us is just amazing. From the comfort of my lounge room chair, I can see into the backyard of our neighbours, whom, you may recall, just happen to be Janine and David. The other day I was gazing out the window and watching David mowing the lawn. My heart just swelled with a warm fuzzy feeling of love and adoration for my loving Heavenly Father, who chose to grant my dear brother-in-law an extension of life.

Such miraculous healing is commonplace in some parts of the broader Church, just as it was in the early Church. It would be wonderful if this was the case in all churches in these latter-days of the Church age. Very sadly and most unfortunately, not everyone we pray for is healed, and we are left asking why.

Another brother-in-law of mine, Andrew's older brother Philip, was diagnosed with cancer toward the end of 2011. Devastatingly, he lost his battle in August 2012 after many months of illness. We also have a five-year-old niece who is currently undergoing treatment after surgery to remove a rare form of cancer in her brain. We continue to earnestly pray for her recovery. The list of loved ones who have battled this insidious disease and other debilitating illnesses could go on.

Why some are healed and others are not is a mystery that is only for God to know the answer to, and we are not to question His wisdom in such. I pray that His Bride may not hinder such miraculous signs and wonders from occurring due to unbelief and lack of obedience to His instruction. I pray that we may all be encouraged by David's incredible story of God's amazing intervention and healing in his life. Sixteen years later, he is still going strong at the time of revising this book.

All praise and honour go to our mighty God. Miracles, signs and wonders do still happen in this day and age!

PART VI

Spiritual Relationships

CHAPTER 16

The Dowry of the Bride

I was interested to note that the two separate words of prophecy spoken over me, as mentioned in chapter thirteen, have both been connected to the reading of God's Word. This is integral to my journey of growing from infancy to knowing intimacy with my Heavenly Husband. As in any marriage relationship, it is not possible to experience genuine love and intimacy with one's partner unless one first gets to know them as a person. How can I expect to experience true intimacy with my Heavenly Husband without first getting to know *Him* as a person? God has provided me with His diary in the form of His Holy Scriptures, the Bible. I get to know Him personally by reading His Word and communing with Him in conversational prayer.

In Genesis chapter four, the word 'knew' is used referring to the act of life-bearing intimacy between Adam and his wife, Eve, and Cain (their son) and his wife. God's perfect plan in marriage is that two beings know each other completely, resulting in the two becoming one being or one flesh. In the natural, this is intimacy in all its fullness.

> Now Adam knew Eve his wife, and she conceived and bore Cain ... (Genesis 4:1).
>
> And Cain knew his wife, and she conceived and bore Enoch ... (Genesis 4:17).
>
> And Adam knew his wife again, and she bore a son and named him Seth ... (Genesis 4:25). (NKJV)

Love and intimacy within a marriage is cultivated as both husband and wife make time and effort to get to know each other. It is the same in my relationship with my Heavenly Husband. Intimacy with God can only be experienced when I make time and effort to get to know Him. It is in knowing Him that I become united as one being with His Holy Spirit. My Heavenly Husband *'knew'* me intimately even before I was conceived in my mother's womb.

> For You formed my inward parts; You covered me in my mother's womb. I will praise You, for I am fearfully and wonderfully made; Marvelous are Your works, And that my soul knows very well. My frame was not hidden from You, When I was made in secret, And skillfully wrought in the lowest parts of the earth.

Your eyes saw my substance, being yet unformed. And in Your book they all were written, The days fashioned for me, When as yet there were none of them (Psalm 139:13-16 NKJV).

God knew everything about me well before I was a twinkle in my parent's eyes. For me, getting to know Him requires a little more effort. He has helped me along somewhat by giving me His 'diary' to read.

The Word of God is a historical account of the creation of the universe and God's purposes and plan of salvation for humanity. It begins with the creation of man and woman in the book of Genesis, where it portrays the reality of a lost Paradise. It then journeys through to the end of humanity's inhabitation of this world, as we know it, and beyond in the book of Revelation, where it portrays the reality of Paradise regained. It contains the prophetic words of the Prophets who spoke of a Saviour who would come to restore Paradise. It is a historical record of the Saviour who came and fulfilled the prophecies.

Many of these factual accounts of history are prophetic by nature, being pictures or blueprints that point to things that once were and to things still to come concerning God's greater purposes for humanity and his destiny pertaining to salvation.

In studying the book of Genesis, I have gleaned more insight into the person of the Holy Spirit, the third person in the Holy Trinity. The Holy Spirit's actively involved in seeking out and preparing the Bride of Christ to meet her Heavenly Husband at the end of this age.

I am referring to the story of Abraham's servant as he searches for a bride for his master's son, Isaac, as found in Genesis 24, the entirety of which I have included below. Being such a long chapter, I debated whether or not to include its entire content, as the dialogue tends to repeat itself to a degree. To get the full picture of the determined pursuit of Abraham's servant of a bride for his master's son, Isaac, you will benefit from reading the whole chapter. However, I have taken the liberty of highlighting in bold the main points of interest that relate to my story. I believe these to be an important part of the message the Lord would have me share with my readers. Remember, the heart of my story is the relationship between the Bride of Christ and her readiness to meet her Bridegroom. Though not necessarily recommended, you may prefer to refrain from reading the whole chapter and simply read the highlighted parts.

Before reading the chapter, it is interesting to note the footnote on page 35 found in the Large Print Amplified Bible about this chapter:

THE DOWRY OF THE BRIDE

This chapter is highly illustrative of God the Father, Who sends forth His Holy Spirit to win the consent of the individual soul to become the bride of His Son. Keep these resemblances constantly in mind as you read and see how the story unfolds. First, meet the Father and note His concern about His Son's bride. Then get acquainted with the Holy Spirit's great, selfless heart, Whose one purpose is to win the girl for His Master's Son. Then meet the Son and note His tenderness as He claims His bride. The longest chapter in Genesis is devoted to this important story.

Genesis 24:1-67

Now Abraham was old, well advanced in age; and the LORD had blessed Abraham in all things. So Abraham said to the oldest servant of his house, who ruled over all that he had, "Please, put your hand under my thigh, and I will make you swear by the Lord, the God of heaven and the God of the earth, that you will not take a wife for my son from the daughters of the Canaanites, among whom I dwell; but **you shall go to my country and to my family, and take a wife for my son Isaac.**"

And the servant said to him, "Perhaps the woman will not be willing to follow me to this land. Must I take your son back to the land from which you came?"

But Abraham said to him, "Beware that you do not take my son back there. The LORD God of heaven, who took me from my father's house and from the land of my family, and who spoke to me and swore to me, saying, 'To your descendants I give this land,' He will send His angel before you, and you shall take a wife for my son from there. And if the woman is not willing to follow you, then you will be released from this oath; only do not take my son back there." So the servant put his hand under the thigh of Abraham his master, and swore to him concerning this matter.

Then the servant took ten of his master's camels and departed, for all his master's goods were in his hand. And he arose and went to Mesopotamia, to the city of Nahor. And he made his camels kneel down outside the city by a well of water at evening time, the time when women go out to draw water. Then he said, "O LORD God of my

master Abraham, please give me success this day, and show kindness to my master Abraham. Behold, here I stand by the well of water, and the daughters of the men of the city are coming out to draw water. Now let it be that the young woman to whom I say, 'Please let down your pitcher that I may drink,' and she says, 'Drink, and I will also give your camels a drink' – let her be the one You have appointed for Your servant Isaac. And by this I will know that You have shown kindness to my master."

And it happened, before he had finished speaking, that behold, Rebekah, who was born to Bethuel, son of Milcah, the wife of Nahor, Abraham's brother, came out with her pitcher on her shoulder. Now the young woman was very beautiful to behold, a virgin; no man had known her. And she went down to the well, filled her pitcher, and came up. And the servant ran to meet her and said, "Please let me drink a little water from your pitcher."

So she said, "Drink, my lord." Then she quickly let her pitcher down to her hand, and gave him a drink. And when she had finished giving him a drink, she said, "I will draw water for your camels also, until they have finished drinking." Then she quickly emptied her pitcher into the trough, ran back to the well to draw water, and drew for all his camels. And the man, wondering at her, remained silent so as to know whether the LORD had made his journey prosperous or not.

So it was, when the camels had finished drinking, that the man took a golden nose ring weighing half a shekel, and two bracelets for her wrists weighing ten shekels of gold, and said, "Whose daughter are you? Tell me, please, is there room in your father's house for us to lodge?"

So she said to him, "I am the daughter of Bethuel, Milcah's son, whom she bore to Nahor." Moreover, she said to him, "We have both straw and feed enough, and room to lodge."

Then the man bowed down his head and worshipped the LORD. And he said, "Blessed be the LORD God of my master Abraham, who has not forsaken His mercy and His truth toward my master. As for me, being on the way, the LORD led me to

THE DOWRY OF THE BRIDE

the house of my master's brethren." So the young woman ran and told her mother's household these things.

Now Rebekah had a brother whose name was Laban, and Laban ran out to the man by the well. So it came to pass, when he saw the nose ring, and the bracelets on his sister's wrists, and when he heard the words of his sister Rebekah, saying, "Thus the man spoke to me," that he went to the man. And there he stood by the camels at the well. And he said, "Come in, O blessed of the LORD! Why do you stand outside? For I have prepared the house, and a place for the camels."

Then the man came to the house. And he unloaded the camels, and provided straw and feed for the camels, and water to wash his feet and the feet of the men who were with him. Food was set before him to eat, but he said, "I will not eat until I have told about my errand."

And he said, "Speak on."

So he said, "I am Abraham's servant. The LORD has blessed my master greatly, and he has become great; and He has given him flocks and herds, silver and gold, male and female servants, and camels and donkeys. And Sarah my master's wife bore a son to my master when she was old; and to him he has given all that he has. Now my master made me swear, saying, 'You shall not take a wife for my son from the daughters of the Canaanites, in whose land I dwell; but you shall go to my father's house and to my family, and take a wife for my son.' And I said to my master. 'Perhaps the woman will not follow me.' But he said to me, 'The LORD, before whom I walk, will send His angel with you and prosper your way; and you shall take a wife for my son from my family and from my father's house. You will be clear from this oath when you arrive among my family; for if they will not give her to you, then you will be released from my oath.'

"And this day I came to the well and said, 'O LORD God of my master Abraham, if You will now prosper the way in which I go, behold, I stand by the well of water; and it shall come to pass that when the virgin comes out to draw water, and I say to her, "Please give me a little water from your pitcher to drink," and she says to me, "Drink, and I will draw for your camels also," – let her be the woman whom the LORD has appointed for my master's son.'

"But before I had finished speaking in my heart, there was Rebekah, coming out with her pitcher on her shoulder; and she went down to the well and drew water. And I said to her, 'Please let me drink.' And she made haste and let her pitcher down from her shoulder, and said, 'Drink, and I will give your camels a drink also.' So I drank, and she gave the camels a drink also. Then I asked her, and said, 'Whose daughter are you?' And she said, 'The daughter of Bethuel, Nahor's son, whom Milcah bore to him.' So I put the nose ring on her nose and the bracelets on her wrists. And I bowed my head and worshipped the LORD, and blessed the LORD God of my master Abraham, who had led me in the way of truth to take the daughter of my master's brother for his son.** Now if you will deal kindly and truly with my master, tell me. And if not, tell me, that I may turn to the right hand or to the left."

Then Laban and Bethual answered and said, "The thing comes from the LORD; we cannot speak to you either bad or good. Here is Rebekah before you; take her and go, and let her be your master's son's wife, as the LORD has spoken."

And it came to pass, when Abraham's servant heard their words, that he worshipped the LORD, bowing himself to the earth. **Then the servant brought out jewelry of silver, jewelry of gold, and clothing, and gave them to Rebekah.** He also gave precious things to her brother and to her mother.

And he and the men who were with him ate and drank and stayed all night. Then they arose in the morning, and he said, "Send me away to my master."

But her brother and her mother said, "Let the young woman stay with us a few days, at least ten; after that she may go."

And he said to them, "Do not hinder me, since the Lord has prospered my way; send me away so that I may go to my master."

THE DOWRY OF THE BRIDE

So they said, "We will call the young woman and ask her personally." Then they called Rebekah and said to her, "Will you go with this man?"

And she said, "I will go."

So they sent away Rebekah their sister and her nurse, and Abraham's servant and his men. And they blessed Rebekah and said to her:

"Our sister, may you become The mother of thousands of ten thousands; And may your descendants possess The gates of those who hate them."

Then Rebekah and her maids arose, and they rode on the camels and followed the man. So the servant took Rebekah and departed.

Now Isaac came from the way of Beer Lahai Roi, for he dwelt in the South. And Isaac went out to meditate in the field in the evening; and he lifted his eyes and looked, and there, the camels were coming. Then Rebekah lifted her eyes, and when she saw Isaac she dismounted from her

camel; for she had said to the servant, "Who is this man walking in the field to meet us?"

The servant said, "It is my master." So she took a veil and covered herself.

And the servant told Isaac all the things that he had done. Then Isaac brought her into his mother Sarah's tent; and he took Rebekah and she became his wife, and he loved her. So Isaac was comforted after his mother's death. (NKJV) [Emphasis mine].

◇◇◇◇◇◇◇◇

This passage is a prophetic picture of how God the Father sent the Holy Spirit into this world to seek a Bride for His Son, Jesus. Many elements of this story of Abraham and his servant, and Rebekah and Isaac, are a picture of God's pursuit of an intimate relationship with His created beings. It also illustrates the process that I must undergo in the choices that need to be made for me to be betrothed to Jesus.

Firstly, we must make the choice to accept God's invitation and say yes to the Holy Spirit's promptings, just as Rebekah was required to accept the servant's invitation and be willing to go with him to meet Isaac as the chosen bride. The servant did not force her to go with him. It was her choice. Abraham instructed his servant that if the woman was unwilling to go with him, he was freed from his obligation.

The servant prayed to God to confirm how the chosen bride should respond to his plea. She must be willing to be of *service* to himself and his camels. I, too, must respond to the Holy Spirit's plea with a willingness to *serve* my master God as I live out my life on this earth.

When the servant said it was time to return to the master, Rebekah's family were reluctant to let her go. It was when Rebekah *said* she was willing to go with the servant that she was released. Rebekah followed the lead of the servant, leaving her family and all that was familiar behind. As the chosen Bride of Christ, I must *confess* my willingness to leave the past behind by repenting of my former ways and by changing my life direction. I willingly and sacrificially follow the Holy Spirit as He leads me to one day meet my Heavenly Husband face to face.

As I have studied this chapter, one thing has caught my attention and caused me to ponder its meaning. It is the significance of the servant giving gifts to the chosen bride, gifts in the form of jewels and garments.

I first refer to the initial gifts given to Rebekah by Abraham's servant in verse 22 of Genesis 24, after Rebekah had actively indicated her willingness to be subject to the servant's request. She willingly served him, becoming a servant herself. In doing so, Abraham's servant was satisfied that she was the chosen bride for his Master's son. He signified this by giving her his initial gift of a nose ring and bracelets. The wearing of these gifts indicated that she was the chosen bride. At this point, Rebekah is destined for her new home, although she and the servant do not leave immediately. The servant dwelt with Rebekah and her family until it was the appointed time to return to the master.

There is a picture unfolding here. Rebekah represents the Church, the chosen Bride of Christ. But what do the jewellery gifts mean concerning you and me, the Bride? Could it be that they represent the gift of the Holy Spirit Himself? In my obedience to the Holy Spirit's promptings, as I willingly express my desire to follow and serve Him, He gives me the initial gift of Himself. He dwells with me until it is the appointed time to return to the Father and meet my Heavenly Husband, Jesus. The Holy Spirit is my seal of approval as the chosen Bride of Christ whilst I remain on this earth. He enters my heart when I accept His proposal of marriage.

Now, what I am about to suggest may seem a little far-fetched, but I am inclined to think that Rebekah's nose ring represents my willingness to be *led* by the Holy Spirit. The Amplified Version of the Bible also mentions an earring as one of the gifts given to Rebekah. This is a reminder to me of my need to be *sensitive to hearing* the voice of the Holy Spirit. The arm bracelets given to Rebekah represent my need to be willing to *use my hands* in His service.

The initial receipt of the gift of the Holy Spirit is a stamp of approval that I have been chosen and called by God to be His Bride. Having fulfilled the requirements - being willing to serve Him as my Lord and Saviour - I am accepted and adopted into God's family. I am an heir and benefactor of God's kingdom. However, it is not yet the appointed time to meet my Heavenly Husband, Jesus. Abraham's servant dwelt with Rebekah and her family until it was time to return to the master. The Holy Spirit is living with me, His chosen Bride, and the rest of His Church, as we await the time to meet Jesus face to face.

I refer to verse 53 of Genesis 24, when Abraham's servant endowed Rebekah with more gifts. A *second blessing*, it would seem. It was nearing when the servant would return to his master with the chosen bride, Rebekah. Her family released her to go. She had indicated her willingness to put her trust in the leading of the servant sacrificially. They were preparing to be on their way to meet her husband, Isaac. At this point in time, as the days of the servant's visit drew to a close, he again endowed Rebekah with silver and gold jewellery and garments of clothing. No doubt such gifts were presented to adorn her in preparation to meet her new husband. It would have been very evident to onlookers that Rebekah was the chosen bride. One could say that these beautiful gift adornments were the dowry she would take with her into the marriage.

As we draw closer to the end of this age, is it possible that the *second blessing of gifts* that the servant presented to Rebekah represents the Holy Spirit's gifts, as spoken of in the following passages?

> There are diversities of gifts, but the same Spirit. There are differences of ministries, but the same Lord. And there are diversities of activities, but it is the same God who works all in all. But the manifestation of the Spirit is given to each one for the profit of all; for to one is given the word of wisdom through the Spirit, to another the word of knowledge through the same Spirit, to another faith by the same Spirit, to another gifts of healings by the same Spirit, to another the working of miracles, to another prophecy, to another discerning of spirits, to another

different kinds of tongues, to another the interpretation of tongues. But one and the same Spirit works all these things, distributing to each one individually as He wills (1 Corinthians 12:4-11 NKJV).

Now you are the body of Christ and members individually. And God has appointed these in the church: first apostles, second prophets, third teachers, after that miracles, then gifts of healings, helps, administrations, varieties of tongues (1 Corinthians 12:27-28 NKJV).

And He Himself gave some to be apostles, some prophets, some evangelists, and some pastors and teachers, for the equipping of the saints for the work of ministry, for the edifying of the body of Christ, till we all come to the unity of faith and of the knowledge of the Son of God, to a perfect man, to the measure of the stature of the fullness of Christ (Ephesians 4:11-13 NKJV)…

Abraham's servant bided his time to endow Rebekah with gifts and garments in preparation to meet her husband, Isaac. In these latter days of the Church age, I wonder whether the Holy Spirit is biding His time, waiting and wanting to fully endow you and me with spiritual gifts and garments in readiness to meet our Husband, Jesus. I fear that we may be at risk of being asleep and not fully endowed with such gifts when the Bridegroom is on His way to meet us. Jesus portrays this unthinkable scenario in His parable of the ten virgins found in Matthew 25:1-13:

> "Then the kingdom of heaven shall be likened to ten virgins who took their lamps and went out to meet the bridegroom. Now five of them were wise, and five were foolish. Those who were foolish took their lamps and took no oil with them, but the wise took oil in their vessels with their lamps. But while the bridegroom was delayed, they all slumbered and slept.
>
> "And at midnight a cry was heard: 'Behold, the bridegroom is coming; go out to meet him!' Then all those virgins arose and trimmed their lamps. And the foolish said to the wise, 'Give us some of your oil, for our lamps are going out.' But the wise answered, saying, 'No, lest there should not be enough for us and you; but go rather to those who sell, and buy for yourselves.' And while they went to buy, the bridegroom came, and those

who were ready went in with him to the wedding; and the door was shut.

"Afterward the other virgins came also, saying, 'Lord, Lord, open to us!' But he answered and said, 'Assuredly, I say to you, I do not know you.'

Watch therefore, for you know neither the day nor the hour in which the Son of Man is coming. (NKJV)

I once thought that this story was referring to believers in Jesus and non-believers. I thought the five wise virgins represented those who believe in Jesus, and the five virgins who were not ready when the bridegroom returned described the non-believers.

It is pretty obvious to me now that all ten virgins were believers in Jesus and His work of salvation, because they were all waiting for the return of the Bridegroom. Quite tragically, though, some of them were not ready when the Bridegroom returned. His words to those left wanting were, *'I do not know you.'* How tragic is that? In other words, they did not *know* Him intimately. They were not well acquainted with Him. They were spiritually immature 'virgins', lacking in relationship and personal knowledge of their Bridegroom. They were waiting to meet Him, yet their lamps of understanding, knowledge and wisdom were empty.

We are told in Psalm 119:105 that God's Word is a *lamp* to our feet and a light to our path. By reading God's Word, we acquire knowledge of Him and get to know Him personally and intimately. Suppose this parable of the ten virgins indicates the percentage of Christians who do not *know God* to the full extent of His will and satisfaction. In this case, 50% of the Church is not ready to meet our Bridegroom. How very tragic!

The *oil* in the lamps of the virgins represents the Holy Spirit. The *evidence* of the Holy Spirit was lacking in their lives. They remained as immature virgins, having become complacent and stagnant in their relationship with their betrothed.

From this passage, it seems that a large proportion of the Church is at risk of not being adequately attired with the gifts and garments of the Holy Spirit when our Bridegroom returns to claim His Bride. We are told that such gifts will be necessary in the last days *'for the equipping of the saints for the work of ministry'* (Ephesians 4:12 NKJV) in preparation for the final harvest, which, according to prophecy, will occur just before the return of our Bridegroom.

I am aware that many in our churches do not believe such a thing as a *second blessing*, referring to a second and ongoing filling or baptism of the Holy Spirit, resulting in manifestations of supernatural gifting and power. Some think that the ministry and gifting of the apostles and the prophets were only relevant to the early Church.

My understanding of the passages above confirms that God intends that the same gifting of the early apostles and prophets would play an ongoing role in the body of Christ. In the early Church, supernatural manifestations of God's power were regular occurrences through the apostles, the prophets, and others. Smatterings of miracles, signs and wonders have continued over the centuries since Christ was on the earth. As we near the end of the age, we will see more miraculous signs and wonders, many of which already occur in some areas of the broader Church.

The miracles, signs and wonders that Jesus performed pointed toward His Father. In these last days that we are currently living in, the granting of such gifts and their purpose point to the glorification of God, not man. They are manifestations of God's power that reveal the heart of the Father toward humanity, to show His love for all. Demonstrating God's love through His gifts will further establish His kingdom here on earth. To fulfil our calling as the Bride of Christ, we must first have faith, believing that God is '... *a rewarder of those who diligently seek Him*' (Hebrews 11:6 NKJV).

As I express my beliefs on this topic, I am conscious that no amount of talking about such things as the gifts of the Spirit will cause them to be manifested in our lives. It is not my place to force my views onto anyone. The Holy Spirit initiates such gifts, distributing them as He so wills. I fear that the Church is oblivious or even choosing to be ignorant of such gifting. There seems to be a lack of desire after the gifts. We do not want our church culture or traditional way of 'doing church' encroached upon, fearing changes we are uncomfortable with. In some churches, anything preached or practised apart from that of traditional evangelical teaching appears to be heresy. I'm not saying that the theology and teachings of your typical evangelical church are incorrect, not by any means. Still, perhaps just a little selective in its teachings, I might dare to say.

I do not intend to be critical of the Church, but has she become comfortable with familiarity? Is she content to be conformed to the way things have always been, content with the selective teaching she knows and understands? I fear that she seems oblivious that certain parts of scripture are avoided due to the belief that they are secondary in importance, even believing that they are irrelevant today.

In expressing my views on this topic, it is not my intent, nor my desire, to cause friction or offence by doing so. I hope and pray that we will be fully prepared to meet our Bridegroom when He returns to take us to Himself. As the betrothed Bride of Christ, is it necessary for us to look at our attire and consider whether we are *'dressed for comfort'*? Or are we dressed in such a fashion that the world will sit up and take notice, if you get my drift? Are *all* the gifts of the Spirit, as noted in the above passages, fully evident and functioning in our churches: *for the edifying of the body of Christ, till we all come to the unity of faith and of the knowledge of the Son of God, to a perfect man, to the measure of the stature of the fullness of Christ?* (Ephesians 4:12-13 NKJV)

Just imagine what an incredible impact we, as the Bride of Christ, could have on this world if we were fully functioning **'to the measure of the stature of the fullness of Christ.'** It seems to me that this will only be possible when the Bride is lavished with all the fruits and gifting(s) of the Holy Spirit.

Referring again to our story in Genesis 24, there is one other gift that the servant gave to Rebekah as she prepared to meet her husband, Isaac. That is the gift of clothes. I believe these represent the clothes of righteous acts of the Bride, administered with love to others in preparation for the return of the Bridegroom, as described in Revelation 19:6-8:

> And I heard, as it were, the voice of a great multitude, as the sound of many waters and as the sound of mighty thunderings, saying, "Alleluia! For the Lord God Omnipotent reigns! Let us be glad and rejoice and give Him glory, **for the marriage of the Lamb has come, and His wife has made herself ready." And to her it was granted to be arrayed in fine linen, clean and bright, for the fine linen is the righteous acts of the saints.** (NKJV) [Emphasis mine].

Also, Isaiah 61:10-11 speaks of a bridegroom and bride prepared for marriage, clothed in garments of salvation and a robe of righteousness.

> I will greatly rejoice in the LORD, My soul shall be joyful in my God; For He has clothed me with the garments of salvation, He has covered me with the robe of righteousness, As a bridegroom decks *himself* with ornaments, And as a bride adorns *herself* with jewels. (NKJV)

What more can I say except to ask the question? Will you and I be ready? Will we be wearing garments of salvation and righteousness, fully endowed and equipped with our dowry of spiritual gifts and clothes of righteous acts when it comes time to meet our Heavenly Husband? Or will we be found wanting, corrupted by earthly treasures, moth-eaten garments and selfish ambitions as portrayed in James 5:1-8?

> Come now, you rich, weep and howl for your miseries that are coming upon you! Your riches are corrupted, and your garments are moth-eaten. Your gold and silver are corroded, and their corrosion will be a witness against you and will eat your flesh like fire. You have heaped up treasures in the last days. Indeed the wages of the labourers who mowed your fields, which are kept back by fraud, cry out; and the cries of the reapers have reached the ears of the Lord of Sabaoth. You have lived on the earth in pleasure and luxury; you have fattened your hearts as in a day of slaughter. You have condemned, you have murdered the just; he does not resist you.
>
> **Therefore be patient, brethren, until the coming of the Lord. See how the farmer waits for the precious fruit of**

> **the earth, waiting patiently for it until it receives the early and latter rain. You also be patient. Establish your hearts, for the coming of the Lord is at hand.** (NKJV) [Emphasis mine].

This passage paints a picture that is relevant to the current times we are living in. James encourages the saints to be patient and establish their hearts, as does the farmer who waits for the latter rain, which precedes the harvest. This is a prophetic picture of the outpouring of the Holy Spirit just before the final harvest of humanity. At the end of the age, Jesus will gather up the elect and take them to be His Bride.

Could the 'latter rain' mentioned in verse seven represent the second outpouring of the Holy Spirit, which is expected to come in the latter-days just before Jesus' return? The 'early rain' would, therefore, refer to the outpouring of the Spirit in the early Church age. During this *second outpouring*, the Church will be endowed with beautiful gifts of the spirit and adorned with beautiful garments of righteous acts. I believe it is beginning to sprinkle. The latter rains are on their way. I am thirsty for this latter rain. Are you?

These beautiful gifts will be useless to the impending harvest if they are not administered with love. Paul instructs us in 1 Corinthians 14:1 to *Pursue love and desire spiritual gifts ...!* (NKJV)

Love and spiritual gifts will only be manifest in my life as I grow in my relationship with my Heavenly Husband. When I spend time in His Word and commune with Him in prayer, I get to know Him as a close friend, counsellor, guide and helper. I am learning to listen for His voice as He speaks and guides my path. I come to know an intimate union with His Holy Spirit and am gradually empowered to be all He would have me be as His Bride, according to His will, not mine.

What a beautiful picture the end of Genesis 24 portrays of the coming together of the bride and bridegroom. Isaac was in the field meditating. He looked up and saw the camels coming, and he set out to meet his bride. Rebekah dismounted from her camel when she saw Isaac coming toward her. She covered herself in humility as she was presented to her betrothed. Isaac took her to his home; she became his wife, and he loved her.

◇◇◇◇◇◇◇◇

Just a note on the writing of this chapter: I sat at my computer well after midnight and on into the early morning hours. I was a little reluctant to write about the 'second blessing', otherwise known as the baptism of the Holy Spirit, knowing that this is a controversial topic in many evangelical churches. I was afraid that my fellow Baptists might take offence. I went to bed feeling uncertain about what the Lord would have me include in this chapter. It was my hope and prayer that He would give me clear thoughts and inspiration in the morning.

I woke up the following day and tuned in to the local Christian radio station to listen to the morning devotions. I heard the messages of two different speakers. One spoke of the passage that I referred to in 1 Corinthians 12, referring to the manifestation of the Spirit through the granting of spiritual gifts. The other referenced the parable of the ten virgins in Matthew 25.

It would seem that the Lord is keen for His Church to hear this message. Is it possible that our lamps (or Bibles, as it were) are gathering dust for lack of use, resulting in us not knowing our Heavenly Husband as we ought? Will Jesus return to find us wanting and lacking in the oil of the Holy Spirit? Rendering us ill-equipped and powerless to fulfil our purpose and calling as the Bride of Christ?

The disturbing part about Jesus' parable of the ten virgins is that not all those waiting for the groom made it to the wedding. No amount of pleading gave them entry to a closed door. They were refused with the words from the bridegroom saying, "I do not *know* you."

I fervently pray that we will all be welcomed into the wedding feast on that glorious day of our Bridegroom's return. We will be ready with our lamps filled to the brim and shining brightly, being well-equipped and empowered due to having known our Heavenly Husband intimately. All for the Glory of our God and His kingdom!

> *'The oil of the Spirit produces Power! The evidence of the Power is in the effectiveness of our service!'* (Author unknown)

CHAPTER 17

Three Equals One

Have you ever tried to wrap your head around the concept of the Holy Trinity? I have to say, it does my head in. If you are not aware, the Trinity is a name the early Christians used to describe God. Though some do not hold to this truth, scripture substantiates that God is actually three persons in one, God the Father, God the Son and God the Holy Spirit. If I claimed to fully understand how this could be possible, I would esteem myself as having a level of intelligence that only belongs to God.

The word Trinity is not actually used in the Bible. This can be a stumbling block to some, believing that the concept of God being three persons in one must, therefore, be false doctrine. Nonetheless, the Bible definitely portrays God as distinctly three divine persons, yet equally one being.

I was thinking about this one day, trying to gain 'some' understanding of how this triune entity is possible and how one can understand what it means, as a Christian, to be spiritually positioned 'in Christ'; both of these concepts being spiritual relationships with multiple components that form 'one' intimate union. It occurred to me that it is a little bit like being on a team. Well, similar, at least. Let's face it, it really is impossible to compare almighty God with anything tangible, quite frankly, but bear with me.

Back in my younger days, I loved playing team sports, especially hockey, netball and basketball. Early in my high-school years, I played on a hockey team that I am proud to say (in a humble sort of way) went through the local competition unbeaten. I attribute our success to the fact that we had a fantastic coach. At training sessions, Mrs Stewart would have us practise running up and down the field, passing the ball across the forward line from one player to the next. Our team played as one body with many different components working together. We all held our positions on the field, and each person had a part to play in reaching the goal. It was essential to keep passing the ball on to another team member. When the opposition attacked, we could offload the ball to another player until we reached the other end of the field, where the one with the first opportunity would score a goal. As in all team sports, we had substitute players standing on the sideline, ready to take the place of fellow team members. For all intents and purposes, the substitute player becomes the person they stand in for, taking over where the other left off and continuing to play the game with the same goal in mind, to be victorious. A team that plays well together, knowing and utilising each other's skills and heeding the coach's instruction, form an intimate bond. Though they are many individuals, they are united as one body with the same objective and purpose.

In the Garden of Eden, God and man were intimately connected in a perfect relationship, doing life together as a team. The perfect union between God and humanity was lost when man and woman decided to please themselves instead of God. They decided to 'play the game of life' independent of their 'coach', which meant the team fell apart. Consequently, you and I have been left up the creek without a paddle, so to speak. (Or on the field without a hockey stick, as it were.) Because of Adam and Eve's disobedience to the 'coach's' instruction, we too, by default, fall short of the standard our 'coach' set for us at the beginning of time, a standard we would need to adhere to be qualified to be on His team.

Thankfully, God the Father came to the rescue by sending His Son Jesus onto this earthly field, making it possible for you and me to be reinstated back onto His team. Jesus became my substitute player, as I am incapable of doing life in a manner that is worthy of being on God's team. Jesus paid the penalty for my imperfections, making it possible for me to get back on His playing field in the kingdom of God once again; to be reunited with my Creator and Coach. Though I was dead in my trespasses, I was made alive again **in Christ**, my substitute. It's as if I literally died on the cross with Jesus and rose again to life with Him. I am a new creation in Christ.

> I have been crucified with Christ; it is no longer I who live, but Christ lives in me; and the life which I now live in the flesh I live by faith in the Son of God, who loved me and gave Himself for me (Galatians 2:20 NKJV).

So, apart from the 'team' analogy, what does it really mean to be 'in Christ?' To even begin to understand this spiritual union, I first need to take a closer look at the Holy Trinity. The role that Jesus plays as a team member of the Holy Trinity qualifies Him to be my substitute, positioning Himself in me and I in Him.

The Holy Trinity - Three in One

God, Himself, is three persons. All three are of equal importance to each other. They make up the institution of the Godhead. They are, in fact, *one being*. They demonstrate perfect intimacy, yet all three persons are individuals. They each have their own purpose within the institution of the Godhead. You can't have one without the other. For example, concerning the salvation of humanity, each person of the Godhead had, and has, a role to play. I will elaborate on this later.

God created man in His image, as is referenced in Genesis 1:26. This verse substantiates well the concept of God being more than one person, yet one God:

> Then **God** said, "Let **Us** make man in **Our** image, according to **Our** likeness; …" (Genesis 1:26 NKJV). [Emphasis mine].

As we are created in God's image, humanity comprises three components: the **soul**, the **body**, and the **spirit**. All three make up the institution of man. Each component is necessary for the makeup of man to sustain life. You can't have one without the other.

It seems that God, being three persons in one Himself, prefers to do things in threes. Each component in man is likened to or typical of each individual person of the Holy Trinity.

The **Father** is the person in the Trinity who is known as the I AM. He is the *soul* or personality of God. He is 'who' God is. God told Moses, referring to Himself, that His name is 'I AM.'

Jesus is the person of the Trinity known as the **Son** who became flesh, or a *body*. It was this component of the Godhead who demonstrated free will. Jesus *chose* to become a sacrifice in the laying down of His life, thereby making it possible again for humanity to have fellowship with God. Jesus submitted to the Father's will.

The **Holy Spirit** is the person in the Trinity who is *spirit* (to state the obvious). He is known as the Servant. He is also known as the helper, the one who imparts life and power.

Both God and man are typically made up of three components: soul, body and spirit. Each member has a role to play in each entity.

The Components that are God

Father	Son	Holy Spirit
Soul / Personality	Body / Flesh	Spirit / Life
Is the Head / Leader.	Is the Choice / Sacrifice.	Is the Servant / Helper.
He exists to Lead and to Love.	He is an 'instrument of choice'.	He exists to Give Life and Empowerment.
	He exists to Honour and Submit.	

The Components that are Man

Soul	Body	Spirit
Personality	Flesh	Life

One In Christ

In all of my deliberating over the make-up of God and man, generally speaking, God is **Spirit**, and man is **flesh**. Yet there is one common denominator between the two. You probably guessed it! *Jesus!* Jesus is both fully God and fully man. When He walked this earth, His relationship with the Father was one of perfect intimacy and union. The Father was in the Son, and the Son was in the Father. They were and are One.

To be 'in Christ' is to be 'one' with Jesus. *He* in me and *I* in Him. Jesus describes this intimate union that applies to His Bride, the Church, when He prays to the Father for those who would believe in Him:

> "I do not pray for these alone, but also for those who will believe in Me through their word; that they all may be one, **as You, Father, are in Me, and I in You**; **that they also may be one in Us**, that the world may believe that You sent Me. And the glory which You gave Me I have given them, **that they may be one just as We are one: I in them, and You in Me**; that they may be **made perfect in one**, and that the world may know that You have sent Me, and have loved them as You have loved Me (John 17:20-23 NKJV). [Emphasis mine].

To be 'in Jesus' is to be in perfect relationship with my Heavenly Husband. That is, to know and love Him personally and to be known and loved by Him. Jesus is my only means of salvation. He is my bridge, or door, by which I may enter back into relationship with the Father. Jesus said ...

> I am the door. If anyone enters by Me, he will be saved ... (John 10:9 NKJV).

> Jesus said to him, "I am the way, the truth, and the life. No one comes to the Father except through Me' (John 14:6 NKJV).

Something of interest took my attention as I thought about Jesus' words. I hadn't considered this before, but once again, God is portrayed as 'three in one': Jesus said 'I AM'... the way ... the truth ... the life.' We know God to be the great I AM as in Exodus 3:14:

> And God said to Moses, "I AM WHO I AM." And He said, "Thus you shall say to the children of Israel, 'I AM has sent me to you.'" (NKJV)

The Great I AM

Son	Father	Holy Spirit
The Way	The Truth	The Life
=	=	=
The Door / The Substitute	The Soul of the I AM	The Manifested Power

I earlier mentioned that the three components of the Godhead, the Holy Trinity, each have a role to play concerning the salvation of man.

The **Father**, the Great 'I AM', being the manifestation of *'Truth,'* came to my rescue by sending His **Son** Jesus to be the *'Way'* to bring me and all of humanity back to Himself. Jesus died a sacrificial death on my behalf as 'my substitute', paying the death penalty for my sins. He rose again to *'Life'* through the 'manifested power' of the **Holy Spirit**.

Another Vision

During the writing of this chapter, in the early hours of the morning, the Lord gave me added insight into what it means to be 'in Christ' by placing the following impression in my mind:

I woke up with a start, having glimpsed a vision of a bottle of milk and a bottle of water. The bottle of milk was tilted and being poured into the bottle of water. As the milk poured out and entered into the bottle of water, the milk turned into a stream of water. The liquid was pouring out as milk but pouring in as water.

I believe the milk represents my immature fleshly nature with all of my spiritually stagnant weaknesses and strivings, and the water represents the Holy Spirit. When I am 'in Christ,' the milk of my flesh becomes one with the Holy Spirit and is manifested into *streams of living water*. I can know the fullness of life in Christ and experience spiritual empowerment that springs up into everlasting life, as depicted in the following passage. Jesus is speaking to the woman of Samaria at the well. She hadn't yet recognised Him as the Christ:

> Jesus answered and said to her, "If you knew the gift of God, and who it is who says to you, 'give Me a drink,' you would have asked Him, and He would have given you living water."

> The woman said to Him, "Sir, You have nothing to draw with, and the well is deep. Where then do you get that living water? Are You greater than our father Jacob, who gave us the well, and drank from it himself, as well as his sons and livestock?"

Jesus answered and said to her, "Whoever drinks of this water will thirst again, **but whoever drinks of the water that I shall give him will never thirst. But the water that I will give him will become in him a fountain of living water springing up into everlasting life**" (John 4:10-14 NKJV). [Emphasis mine].

The *living water* that Jesus speaks of here is the *Holy Spirit*. To be 'in Christ' is to have the Holy Spirit living in me. To be 'in Christ' is to **'be one'** with, and on the same team as the Holy Trinity:

God the *Father* is my **head coach**. He oversees my life and instructs me through His Word. My coach has an ordained purpose and plan for me, with the intent that I achieve the goals set before me. He is in charge. He is with me, albeit on the sideline as it were, watching over all that plays out, cheering me on in this game of life.

God the *Son* is my **perfect substitute**. I am not capable of playing a 'perfect' game on my own. Only 'in Him' and because of His righteousness am I qualified to play on God's team.

God the *Holy Spirit* is my **source of empowerment**. He develops in me the fruits of His Spirit and grants to me spiritual gifts of power, equipping me to fulfil my purpose and ultimately score the winning goal in this game of life.

There ends my attempt to explain the concept of the Holy Trinity, and what it means to be in Christ, both being entities comprising multiple individuals that together form one intimate union.

I must admit, mathematics was never my best subject at school. Still, I am pretty sure that one, plus one, plus one, never ever amounted to 'one'!

But when it comes to the Holy Trinity and being in Christ…trust me…with God…all things are possible!

CHAPTER 18

And the Two Shall Become One

And the Lord God caused a deep sleep to fall on Adam, and he slept; and He took one of his ribs, and closed up the flesh in its place. Then the rib which the Lord God had taken from man He made into a woman, and He brought her to the man.

And Adam said:

> "This is now bone of my bones
>
> And flesh of my flesh;
>
> She shall be called Woman,
>
> Because she was taken from Man."

Therefore a man shall leave his father and mother and be joined to his wife, and they shall become one flesh (Genesis 2:21-24 NKJV).

At the risk of complicating matters even further in this day and age of 'marriage equality', dare I suggest that God's intent when initiating the institution of marriage was that it would consist of **three** components? (You may at this point be scratching your head thinking ... hang on, according to the above passage of scripture, there can only be two people in a marriage. Three would be a little crowded!)

You are correct! Yet, I believe God Himself would have it, that 'He' be the third person in a marriage relationship consisting of one man, one woman, and one God in the form of His Holy Spirit, forming one intimate union. Each 'person' (or component) within the union has a role to play for the marriage to function as God intended, just as in the institutions of God and man. I suspect some of you may not be comfortable with what I am about to present concerning the roles of the man and woman. If this is the case, you will need to read the whole chapter before jumping to conclusions.

The Components of Marriage

Man	Woman	Holy Spirit
Is Head / Leader	Is Choice / Submission	Is Servant / Helper
He exists to Lead and to Love.	She is an 'Instrument of Choice'. She exists to Honour and Submit.	He exists to Give Life and Empowerment.

Feeling a degree of indignation by any chance? *No man is going to lord it over me!* you may be thinking.

On the day that Andrew and I were married, I understood that God's ideal for marriage is that the husband would be the head of the family. I have always been pleased and willing for this to be the case. I did not see this to be an insult to my intelligence or worth as a person. It is simply the role that God would have him step into in committing to our marriage.

My role is to be my husband's helper. It is up to me to stand alongside him so that we can work together as a team. He is to be open to my opinions and consider me as his equal. I am to contribute in whatever way I can to support him in his role as the head of our marriage and as the head of our family. It is my role to esteem him, giving him honour and respect as he endeavours to fulfil his God-given role as the head.

> And the Lord God said, "It is not good that man should be alone; I will make him a **helper comparable** to him" (Genesis 2:18 NKJV). [Emphasis mine].

When God gave Andrew the responsibility of being the head of our relationship, He did not give him the right to lord over me as a dictator. God's intent was that Andrew would lead out of love and consideration for me and my needs. He is to take on the likeness of God the Father, just as He is the head of the Holy Trinity. He is to rule and lead from a place of love.

At the end of this age, when all is said and done, humanity will bow to God's sovereignty and rule. He will be (and is now) the King of kings and Lord of lords. In the meantime, even though not every person on earth acknowledges His ruler-ship, He still remains sovereign over His creation and always will be. Yet, in His sovereignty, He chose to give humanity free will. He gave me the ability to *choose* whether or not to come under His rule as I live out my days on this earth.

And so it is with me as Andrew's wife. When God created me as an 'Instrument of Choice' being of the female species, He gave me the ability to choose whether or not to come under Andrew's rule and leadership as my husband. Suppose I were ignorant of God's intent for me. I could lord over my husband by being demanding and manipulative, insisting in my own way. But instead, by choosing to submit to Andrew's intents and purposes as my husband, I give him respect and honour. I profess to not having always perfected this in my relationship with my husband. Still, in submission, I choose to place his needs before my own to the best of my ability, limited as that may be. I submit to his leadership because I desire to love and serve Andrew as my husband. Andrew, in turn, oversees our relationship out of love for me, wishing to serve me as his wife, with my best interest at heart. He will not demand more of me than I can give.

Success in a marriage is all about two people demonstrating the servant heart of Christ. It's about putting the needs of your spouse before your own needs, submitting one to the other.

God's concept of marriage is perfect, yet His laws and ideals are not always heeded, thus the high percentage of breakdown in marriage relationships. Many enter into marriage with the mind that they can always get a divorce if things don't work out. That's if they even choose to marry in the first place. The trendy thing to do these days is to try before you buy. There is a fear of commitment for many, or so it would seem.

Whatever happened to the good old days when 'Love and marriage went together like a horse and carriage,' as the old song goes? This is a totally foreign concept for many in this day and age. I remember having a conversation with a young girl many years ago. She had been in and out of several relationships. I expressed to her my belief that sex was designed to take place within the confines of marriage. She was blown away by such a suggestion, having never considered such a 'foreign' concept before. I believe this girl had several step brothers and sisters, most of them having different mothers. Good morals and commitment to marriage had not been modelled well for this young girl. Such dysfunction in families is commonplace these days and almost even considered to be the norm. Is it any wonder that God's ideal of marriage has seemingly gone almost entirely out the window? This lack of moral standing is passed on through the generations and is becoming more and more prolific with every child born. The increase in our society of dysfunctional families is only adding to the degeneration of humanity as we approach the end of the age.

According to the above scripture in Genesis chapter two, when God created man and woman, His perfect plan was that the two would become one flesh. That they would be united in marriage forever, 'until death, do they part'.

To the detriment of us all, we sadly live in a fallen world. I completely acknowledge that some marriages simply are not a healthy union. A divorce is a necessary option that many will resort to. Moses, in fact, permitted that man could write a certificate of divorce, yet Jesus explains the reasoning for this in Mark 10: 5 - 9:

> And Jesus answered and said to them, "Because of the hardness of your heart he wrote you this precept. But from the beginning of creation, God 'made them male and female.' 'For this reason a man shall leave his father and mother and be joined to his wife,

and the two shall become one flesh'; so then they are no longer two, but one flesh. Therefore what God has joined together, let no man separate." (NKJV)

We can be grateful that God is gracious and forgiving when we acknowledge our downfalls, when marriage doesn't work out according to His 'perfect' plan. Yet, when two people have become *one flesh,* and the relationship is fractured for whatever reason, a considerable sense of loss will occur. A severing of one's very soul, I believe. Such a loss will feel as if a part of yourself has been taken from you. Those who have experienced divorce, or lost a life-long partner after many years of marriage, would know the reality of this truth. Still, God's perfect plan was that two people would become one flesh, committing to one person for life.

When He created man and woman, God's ideal was that they would be partners and become one person, as it were, 'knowing' each other intimately. Perfect and complete intimacy between two people is the act of giving one's whole *self* over to another for life.

When One Flesh becomes Double Trouble

I was at the clothesline this morning when it suddenly occurred to me that the words 'flesh' and 'self' have the same letters, except for one. In fact, 'self' is 'flesh' spelt backwards without the 'h'. The two are very closely related, it would seem.

This got me thinking. In the very first chapter of this book, you may recall that I shared with you how a marriage relationship may be impacted by the onslaught of menopause, causing a lack of intimacy within a marriage. I concluded that the reasoning for this lack of intimacy was due to the fact that:

'The *desires* and *intent* of a loving husband are undermined and thwarted by his bride's *battle* with the *flesh*.'

In this context, the 'flesh' was the cause of the problem. In fact, as my book unfolded, this 'battle with the *flesh*' became one of the central themes. As I have resolved to have a play with words, one could replace the word 'flesh' in the above statement with the word 'self', and it would mean the same thing. This battle with the flesh that I have frequently made reference to in this book, diagnosed as being spiritually menopausal, or spiritually stagnant, is in actual fact, a battle with one's own self.

God's intent in initiating the marriage union was that the husband and wife would become one *flesh*. In this context, the *flesh* is portrayed as something beautiful. Two beings becoming one *flesh* is intimacy personified. This is the way God intended it to be initially, at the time of creation.

Unfortunately, the *self* reared its ugly head. Adam and Eve's focus on their own *self-promotion* caused a fracture in the perfect intimate relationship that God had designed and created.

God had created the flesh of man and woman to be something perfect and beautiful. But instead, it was manipulated and turned around, becoming the imperfect self. It changed from something perfect into being something to contend with. When two 'selfs' come together in marriage, both having their own interests at heart, you may end up with double trouble instead of one beautiful flesh.

Ok, so to continue my possibly annoying deliberations, flesh written backwards is self without the 'h'. This got me thinking. Where does the 'h' fit into the whole scheme of things? How do we turn the self back into its original form of perfect flesh, utilising the letter 'h' again?

Light bulb moment! It occurred to me that 'h' is the first letter of the word 'holy'. Put this together with 'self' and you end up with 'holy self'. How about that? Problem solved! Well, not quite. We need a complete transformation to take place so that our self becomes holy again, getting us back to where God intended us to be in the first place; perfectly holy as He is Holy.

Unfortunately, words on the page do not truly address the issue at hand. A complete transformation needs to take place for my 'self' to actually become holy. Only through the sanctifying power of the Holy Spirit working in me, as I abide in Christ and He in me, will my *flesh* be slowly transformed, gradually becoming more Christ-like, instead of being an enemy that I constantly do battle with.

Ideally, both husband and wife will be 'in Christ' and fully yielded to Him when it comes to marriage. They are empowered by the working of the Holy Spirit to develop in their characters the attributes of Jesus, that of love, submission and self-sacrifice; enabling them both to fulfil their role and purpose in their marriage relationship.

We would all do well to heed the advice given to us by the apostle Paul in Ephesians 5:22-33:

> Wives, submit to your own husbands, as to the Lord. For the husband is head of the wife, as also Christ is head of the church; and He is the Savior of the body. Therefore, just as the church is subject to Christ, so let the wives be to their own husbands in everything.
>
> Husbands, love your wives just as Christ also loved the church and gave Himself for her, that He might sanctify and cleanse her with the washing of water by the word, that He might

present her to Himself a glorious church, not having spot or wrinkle or any such thing, but that she should be holy and without blemish. So husbands ought to love their own wives as their own bodies; he who loves his wife loves himself. For no one ever hated his own flesh, but nourishes and cherishes it, just as the Lord does the church. For we are members of His body, of His flesh and of His bones. "For this reason a man shall leave his father and mother and be joined to his wife, and the two shall become one flesh." This is a great mystery, but I speak concerning Christ and the church. Nevertheless let each one of you in particular so love his own wife as himself, and let the wife see that she respects her husband. (NKJV)

What more can I say? That passage says it all, really! Marriage is a beautiful union of one man and one woman becoming one flesh. Ordained by God to illustrate what it means to be one with Christ, my Heavenly Husband. I submit to His ruler-ship by honouring Him and sacrificially giving my life to Him. Jesus, in turn, sanctifies and cleanses me with His Word and the work of His Holy Spirit. I am slowly but surely transformed from my spiritually stagnant state of fleshly struggles into a glorious Bride that will one day be without spot or wrinkle or any such thing. Destined to be beautiful and pure, holy and without blemish.

CHAPTER 19

The Root of all Evil is Self

When I accepted Jesus into my life as my Lord and Saviour, I effectively committed my life to Him in Spiritual marriage. God is my Heavenly Father, yet He is also my Heavenly Husband, having entered into a covenant relationship with Him.

The earthly institution of marriage is typical of the spiritual covenant between God and His creation, the way it was in the beginning of time before man fell out of relationship with God. God's design for earthly and spiritual marriage is that two beings would unite as one, an intimate union where each person gives themselves over entirely to the other. As already discussed in the previous chapter, God's ideal for marriage is perfect. Yet, there is one major problem when trying to execute God's perfect will, and that is **self**!

In God's Word, we are told that the love of money is the root of all kinds of evil. In my opinion, the love of money would not exist without there first being a misappropriated love of self. This inclination to be self-focused does not make for an easy transition when entering a marriage relationship.

As carnal human beings, humanity has an inbuilt tendency to be self-centred and selfish. This trait began when we were in that 'terrible twos' stage of life, when we thought that everything we fancied had our name on it. For the average preschool age child, the word 'share' is not comprehensible, as if being derived from a foreign language. The whole concept that one cannot have *everything* one wants in life, to keep for oneself, just does not compute.

This unfortunate trait of humanity stems from the beginning of time when Adam and Eve decided to do things their way instead of God's way. As soon as they had eaten the forbidden fruit, they suddenly became very self-focused. It was Adam and Eve's selfish ambitions that caused the problem in the first place. When they chose to please themselves instead of pleasing God, their self-centredness suddenly turned into self-consciousness. They went from being naked without any qualms whatsoever to ducking for cover due to total embarrassment, suddenly being aware that they had no clothes on.

Not only were they ducking for cover from embarrassment, but they were also in fear of God's wrath, having disobeyed His commands. Not only did they suddenly find themselves to be naked, but they were also suddenly very much aware of their sinfulness before a righteous God, a God who is intent on holiness and obedience to His Word. They suffered the consequences of their self-seeking pride. They were cast away from His presence, resulting in severing their relationship with God. Not only were *they* banished from His presence, but the rest of humanity are also now suffering the consequences of Adam and Eve's self-indulgences. We have inherited their bent on being self-focused.

Most people who walk this planet have, at some stage of life, experienced either too high an opinion of themselves or too low an opinion of themselves (self included). We may suffer from an over-abundance of pride, feeling as though the world owes us everything there is to be had in this life, feeling a need to keep up with the Joneses, and so on. Or we may be bogged down in self-doubt and inferiority issues, feeling as though we don't quite hit the mark or measure up to the world's standards; this trait also being a form of pride.

Some can be somewhat self-centred, focusing on their own self-gratification and selfish ambition. There are times when some may even feel a degree of self-righteousness or just plain selfishness. Sometimes we may feel just downright sorry for ourselves. All such traits basically amount to the same thing, and that is, an over-abundance of pride and self-focus. Our lives are ordered to some extent, and our destiny is influenced by how much we focus on our own self-interest.

An over-abundance of focus on one's *self* could be classified as a form of idolatry. If I were to esteem myself as capable of living independent of God and His plan for me, I would actually be placing my trust in my own ability to fulfil my purpose and destiny, as was the case with Adam and Eve. I would place my own self-interests before God's. This, in my opinion, is a form of idolatry. Idolatry and selfish ambition are an abomination to God.

> Now the works of the flesh are evident, which are: adultery, fornication, uncleanness, lewdness, **idolatry**, sorcery, hatred, contentions, jealousies, outbursts of wrath, **selfish ambitions**, dissensions, heresies, envy, murders, drunkenness, revelries, and the like; of which I tell you beforehand, just as I also told you in time past, **that those who practice such things will not inherit the kingdom of God** (Galatians 5:19-21 NKJV). [Emphasis mine].

Those are pretty harsh words that 'those who practice such things will not inherit the kingdom of God!' Thank the Lord for His saving grace and work of salvation is all I can say to that!

THE ROOT OF ALL EVIL IS SELF

I must admit that a large portion of my issues in life have stemmed from an *over-abundance of self-focus*. For me, it is more a case of having feelings of inferiority and self-doubt and lacking self-confidence rather than having an issue with overt pride of entitlement or self-seeking.

I suffered depression over the years primarily because I was consumed with my own self-interests. My focus was on the things in my life that impacted me negatively, resulting in me feeling sorry for myself.

Had I not been so obsessed with the opinions of others and what people might think of me, I could have breezed through primary school wearing *short* socks. I probably would have enjoyed the four years of my hairdressing apprenticeship a lot more had I not been so self-conscious and lacking in self-confidence. Not to mention the forty-plus years of hairdressing since! Suppose I hadn't compared myself to my many cousins, many of whom went on to further education, becoming teachers, doctors, occupational therapists, lawyers, journalists, computer technicians, nurses, psychologists and psychiatrists, among other esteemed careers. In this case, I might not have been so down on myself. I had always felt as though I was behind the door when brains were handed out, so to speak.

Despite my fleshly attributes, I am most valuable in God's eyes, as are you and all of God's creation. He created me in His image with the intent that I would take on His characteristics and nature of love and self-sacrifice. My obsessions with self, from whatever perspective, prevent me from being the person God intended me to be. I cannot display God's nature of love for others, putting the interests of others before my own, when I am totally focused on myself.

Jesus did not have a selfish or self-centred bone in His body. Despite our many flaws, He was prepared to sacrifice His own life for ours. His love for us is immeasurable.

> But God demonstrates His own love toward us, in that while we were still sinners, Christ died for us (Romans 5:8 NKJV).

God's love for me is not dependent on my righteous acts or how good a person I am, nor who I perceive myself to be. He died for me despite my sinful fleshly attributes and ways. He was prepared to give up His life in *self-sacrifice,* thereby bridging the gap between a righteous God and a sinful self-indulgent person. In so doing, He made it possible for me to come once again into His Holy presence. He made it possible for me to know *intimacy* with Him as my Heavenly Husband.

In this day and age, marriage relationships are falling apart at an ever-increasing number and rate. Would it be fair to assume that this is due mainly to an over-abundance of self-focus on the part of individuals? In a generation whose motto is 'look out for number one,' I need to be reminded that Christ did not please Himself. He did not come to be served but to serve. Jesus said:

> And whoever desires to be first among you, let him be your slave – just as the Son of Man did not come to be served, but to serve, and to give His life a ransom for many (Matthew 20:27-28 NKJV).

Overcoming the temptations of this world and those of my own fleshly inclinations of self-gratification etc. is no easy feat. Yet, Jesus, even in His humanness, managed to do just that. Not only did He deny Himself, but He lived for others.

> Then Jesus said to His disciples, "If anyone desires to come after Me, let him deny himself, and take up his cross, and follow Me. For whoever desires to save his life will lose it, but whoever loses his life for My sake will find it" (Matthew 16:24-25 NKJV).

There was a time when I misunderstood the intent of this passage. I used to think that the 'taking up of one's cross' referred to the burdens we face in life. I thought it meant that I must endure the carrying of my burdens, just as Jesus was burdened under the weight of the cross He carried. I now see this passage in a different light.

I have come to understand that the 'taking up of one's cross' means that I am to *submit* to the power of what the Cross represents; that is a laying down or denying of oneself. The Cross is a place of execution. As I put to death my own selfish will and inclinations of the flesh, I begin to be regenerated into the person God intended me to be.

> Do nothing out of selfish ambition or vain conceit, but in humility consider others better than yourselves. Each of you should look not only to your own interests, but also to the interests of others.

> Your attitude should be the same as that of Christ Jesus:

> Who, being in very nature God, did not consider equality with God something to be grasped, but made himself nothing, taking the very nature of a servant, being made in human likeness. And being found in appearance as a man, he humbled himself and

became obedient to death – even death on a cross! Therefore God exalted him to the highest place and gave him the name that is above every name, that at the name of Jesus every knee should bow, in heaven and on earth and under the earth, and every tongue confess that Jesus Christ is Lord, to the glory of God the Father (Philippians 2:3-11 NIV).

God's solution to the breakdown of relationships is to recreate man and woman in His own likeness. I became a *new creation in Christ* when I was spiritually born again through belief and faith in Jesus' self-sacrifice on the Cross. He paid the penalty for my sinful fleshly ways. From this mysterious positioning of being *in Christ*, I am empowered by His indwelling Holy Spirit. I am gradually being regenerated and transformed into the likeness of Jesus.

My covenant relationship(s) of marriage, both in the physical and spiritual, will be as God intended them to be as I learn to submit to the power of the Holy Spirit; as I grow to imitate Christ's willingness to serve others instead of overtly serving my own self. God's ideal intent and purpose concerning the covenant of earthly marriage is that it would be a perfect union of two beings, male and female, both serving each other in self-sacrifice.

CHAPTER 20

It's all about Relationship

Even through the writing of this book, God has been teaching me that intimacy within a covenant relationship can only come from a place of serving, the handing over of one's self to another. Intimacy also comes from a place of knowledge, of knowing another and being known in return. As I have served my God in the writing of this book, I have gained further knowledge and understanding of who He is.

Yet, in saying that, I cannot begin to fully understand or comprehend God and all that there is to know about Him. The complexity of His creation, the world and the universe beyond are so unfathomable. I am just a tiny little speck compared to the immense enormity of God's creation. I don't even have words to describe His Majesty and Glory, yet He takes time to be concerned about little old me who has 'stagnancy' issues, both physically and spiritually.

To put things into perspective, my 'issues' are of little significance to the trauma and devastation that the world is experiencing in this day and age.

Because of the injustices surrounding us from every side, it seems, many do not believe in God. Or they may acknowledge that He exists, but they wonder how a so-called loving God could allow a young child to contract cancer. They wonder why so many millions of people suffer due to famine and wars. They wonder how a loving God could allow loved ones to suffer illness and be taken from us way before their time. And why innocent people are killed in car accidents. The list could go on and on.

I have defended God and His love for us on many occasions, blaming the world's chaos on the fall of man. God is not the author of hatred and destruction. He is a loving God. I know this to be true by experience. Yet, He is a God to be feared. He is a God to be revered. He is a God to be honoured. He is a God who demands justice. He is a jealous God who will not tolerate idolatry, the worship of other gods before Himself. He is a God to be esteemed to the full measure of His majesty and power. Yet, the world has chosen to ignore Him and wrongfully blame Him. The world has gone about its business, turning a blind eye to the very Being who holds the universe in place. The world chooses to live independent of God, only acknowledging His existence when something terrible happens. Then it is often only to lay blame.

Very sadly, many in this world do not even *know* Him. They don't *know* His heart. They don't *know* His intent and purposes for their existence. They don't *know* that He loves them more than words can express. He gave up His very life for them, yet they turn a blind eye, continuing to hold Him to blame and acknowledge Him only from a distance.

Many are troubled by the state of the world, wondering what the solution is, but it does not seem to occur to them to look to God for answers. The solutions and purpose for life itself are only found in knowing the God who created the universe through reading His Word.

Some look to themselves for self-fulfilment and purpose. Others esteem the many false prophets who have lived through the ages who claim to know 'truth' and 'enlightenment.' Some even consider Jesus equal only to the rest of the prophets, gleaning from the benefits of His teaching. Yet, their eyes are blinded to the truth of who He really is because they do not *know* Him.

Down through the ages, there have been many false prophets and many false gods in this world. It has been said that all religions point to one God. Those of this belief are sadly misguided. The world has come up against a movement whose goal is to destroy all who do not come under submission to their god. Their god is *not* my God. The God that I know has a heart of love and justice, not of evil and injustice.

IT'S ALL ABOUT RELATIONSHIP

We are created with an inbuilt yearning to know the truth. According to 'Google,' there are over 4000 different religions around the world. Millions of people look to such religious groups to find truth, fulfilment, meaning and purpose in life.

Christianity is the only 'religion' that serves a God who has conquered death. Jesus rose to life and ascended to heaven to take up His position at the right hand of the Father. He *is* alive! The factual truth of His death and resurrection is substantiated well, both in scripture and in historical records. Many have tried to disprove the resurrection of Jesus and have failed. In so doing, they have actually converted to the faith.

Christianity is the only 'religion' that is not about 'religion.' Christianity is all about **relationship**! It's all about a relationship with the one true God. His entire creation, and that includes you and me, came into being for His good pleasure. Yet, many in this world esteem Him not!

Some even call themselves Christians, but they do not truly desire and seek to know God. Many *religiously* sit in our church pews every Sunday, claiming salvation from eternal condemnation through the shed blood of Jesus, yet they are seemingly content to leave it at that. They embrace 'religion' for the sake of religiosity and even out of fear of death and beyond. Still, they apparently have no regard for the relationship that is *at the heart* of Christianity. Are we passive and lukewarm Christians having just enough faith in Jesus to be saved? Or are we passionately in love with our Heavenly Husband, desiring with all our heart to know Him more and more each day, waiting expectantly for His return to earth to take us to be with Him forever?

God is a good and loving Father who longs for a relationship with His creation. His very nature and being are such that He cannot tolerate evil. A loving father disciplines his children, allowing them to suffer the consequences of disobedience. So too, our loving Heavenly Father allows us to suffer the consequences of our disobedience to His instruction. He disciplines out of love, desiring that we would turn from our wicked ways and grow to be more like Him, but many see His chastening to be hateful. As a loving father deserves honour and respect, so much more so does He.

We can be very thankful that He is a patient God, though He will not hold back the *full* extent of His wrath forever. The time is coming fast when we will be required to stand before Him and give an account of our lives. Have we held Him in the place of honour He deserves? Have we taken the time to get to know Him personally? Do we even possess a Bible, let alone read it? Do we have any understanding whatsoever of why God created us in the first place?

I pray with all my heart that as you have read through the pages of this book, you may be a little more aware of God and His loving heart. He simply wants you to know and love Him for who He truly is.

I am amazed at His complexity, yet His purpose for creation is really very simple. He is an intimate Being who longs to know intimacy with His created beings. He has designed *us* to be intimate beings with a need to belong. He initiated the marriage institution between a man and a woman in His likeness, being one perfect union. His desire and intent is that marriage would be a sacred union where we can know what it means to be loved and belong. Within the sanctity of marriage, we gain a better understanding of who God is, His divine intent being that relationships are based on the firm foundation of Love.

God *is* love! When God is taken out of the equation of life, what do we have left? We have a world that has gone crazy. We have a world full of hatred, evil and confusion. We have a world that has taken the God-ordained institution of marriage and turned it into a sham. We have a world that has no respect for human life and has legalised the killing of babies in the womb. We have a world where people kill their fellow man in the name of 'their' god. We have a world where male and female are no longer recognised as such. We have a world where biblical and moral standards have been turned upside down, where what was once morally 'right' and accepted as such is now considered to be 'wrong'. And what was once morally 'wrong' is now considered 'right'. Truth has become lies and lies have become truth. We have a world where Christians who stand up for their beliefs and their right to be heard as Christians are blatantly persecuted and labelled as intolerant haters of those who oppose their views when in actual fact, it is the other way around. Instead, the world has become intolerant of Christians and all that they stand for. May the Lord have mercy on us all!

My God is a gentleman. He did not *force* Himself into my life. He gave me freewill to *choose* for myself to acknowledge Him and learn to love Him. True love can only be satisfying to both parties when it is reciprocated by choice, not force.

Intimacy with my creator God is not found in empty religion. The purpose for living is not found within my own self-promotion or attempting to gain fulfilment in the ways of this world. Purpose for living can only be found in *knowing* the one and only true God. It's *all* about relationship!

CHAPTER 21

The Heavenly Husband and His Latter Day Bride

For your Maker is your husband, The Lord of hosts is His name; And your Redeemer is the Holy One of Israel; He is called the God of the whole earth (Isaiah 54:5 NKJV).

The writing of this book came about because the Lord gave me the original title, *Menopause and the Latter Day Bride* in a vision. It took me a little while to figure out what He would have me derive from this topic. Just as my life is a work in progress, so too has been the journey of this book. With each publication, this being the third, I have made changes along the way, yet the main theme has remained the same.

I had been a Christian for many years, knowing assurance of my salvation by God's grace, yet my relationship with my Heavenly Husband had stagnated, causing me to feel unfulfilled, unproductive and lacking in power. I believed there was much more to be experienced as a child of the living God and as a chosen Bride of Christ. I wondered what was missing in my spiritual journey, causing me to feel less than I should be as a Christian.

It eventually became evident through a not-so-subtle hint from the Lord that I was suffering from *Spiritual Menopause*. A proverbial stagnancy and blockage in my growth as a Christian kept me from being the holy Bride God intended me to be. This weakness in my flesh manifested itself in the following allegorised symptoms:

Hot Flush / Temperature Fluctuations –There were times when I would be *on fire* for the Lord, knowing a close and warm sense of union with His Spirit. Then, randomly and without warning, usually due to life's circumstances, I felt like I was left out in the cold. My relationship with my Heavenly Husband had fizzled to a cold dying ember, leaving me with a sense of loss as though He had inadvertently removed me from His presence.

Insomnia / Restlessness – I could not *rest* in knowing that God loves me and knows my every need, and oversees every aspect of my life. My inability to relax and to *rest in Him* left me grappling with worry, fear and anxiety. I lacked in knowing the abiding peace and presence of Jesus, instead feeling 'afflicted…, tossed with tempest, and not comforted' (Isaiah 54:11 NKJV).

Lacking Clarity / Dulled Hearing – I was taught from a young age that the Holy Spirit would be my counsellor and guide. Yet, I did not know how to hear or recognise His voice. I could not determine His will for my life and what direction I should go. My life was like stagnant water in a blocked drain pipe, gurgling around looking for direction, unable to flow and confidently move forward.

Depression / Depressed Spirit – For many years, I lived under the bondage of a *spirit of heaviness*, feeling downcast and defeated under a cloud of darkness. I was vulnerable to Satan's attack, and he delighted in keeping me bound in spiritual and physical bondage.

Memory Loss / Complacency – Even though I read my Bible regularly, I could not retain God's Word in my memory for very long. I *lacked discipline* in memorising scripture due to *complacency* and *laziness*. I could not confidently recall and speak out God's Word when faced with opposition and the enemy's lies.

Vagueness / Ill-defined Identity – Despite my being a Christian for many years, a *vague* and *poor understanding* of my *true identity in Christ* left me ill-equipped and powerless to overcome life's struggles. I felt defeated and even burdened with guilt when faced with spiritual and fleshly battles.

Fatigue / Dormant Mind – A blocked mindset kept me from maturing and moving forward in my faith due to a slave-to-the-flesh mentality. I believed I could never be holy until I was promoted to heaven. I was fatigued and frustrated in my spiritual walk as I tended to rely on my fleshly nature for empowerment. I would strive in my own strength, rather than relying on the power of the Holy Spirit to transform me into the person God would have me be, and that is pure and lovely, portraying 'The Beauty of Holiness'.

Just as a woman is subject to the debilitating effects of menopause in her latter years of life, I was spiritually menopausal in these latter days of the Church age. I knew that Jesus loved me despite my weak and fleshly condition, but I was conscious of falling short when it came to fulfilling the desires of my Heavenly Husband. As a result, I, too, was unfulfilled. I was rendered barren due to my spiritually menopausal and stagnant condition, unable to produce the seed-bearing fruit that would give honour and glory to my Heavenly Husband.

The Lord created me with an inherent need to be loved and to feel secure in relationship. He designed the institution of marriage so that from a human perspective, my needs can be met within my earthly relationship with my husband. And so it is in my relationship with my Heavenly Husband. I am so grateful for the Lord's love and gentle nurturing in all my struggles over the years. He knew of my heartfelt desire to be close to Him, wanting desperately to be the person He would have me be. The trouble was that I was relying on *my* ability to be that person, striving in my own strength to change my ways without success. As much as I loved my Lord and was committed to Him, I just could not understand where I was going wrong. Slowly but surely, with the gentle nurture of the Holy Spirit, I eventually came to realise what was missing in my relationship with my Heavenly Husband, and that was **intimacy!**

Knowing intimacy with my God is the all-important remedy for every one of my spiritually menopausal symptoms. As I: *dwell in the secret place of the Most High,* [*and*] *abide under the shadow of the Almighty* (Psalm 91:1 NKJV), I find a beautiful place of refuge.

No longer does my spiritual thermostat fluctuate between 'hot flushes' and 'cold embers'. I remain, instead, in the place of warmth and security as I *shelter beneath the wings* of my God, my Heavenly Husband.

Insomnia and restlessness are no longer a major problem, once having grappled with worry, fear and anxiety. I rest so much easier when I simply hand my troubles over to my Lord, relaxing and resting in the comfort and peace of knowing that He loves me intimately and will tend to my every need.

I am slowly but surely gaining confidence in hearing God's voice, the gentle whisper of the Holy Spirit as He guides me on this path of life, giving me more clarity in knowing what direction I should take when faced with life's decisions.

I no longer suffer from 'depression,' being bound by Satan under a cloud of darkness. I stand completely protected as I daily put on my armour that is Jesus Himself. In doing so, I am covered and saved by His righteousness, His peace, His faith, His salvation, and the sword of His Spirit, which is His Word. To further secure my protection, I regularly put on a 'garment of praise' to keep the insidious spirit of heaviness at bay.

I no longer suffer from 'memory loss' due to complacency that kept me from diligently studying and memorising God's Word. The more passionate I am to know my Lord through His Word, the more His Word gives me a passion for knowing my Heavenly Husband more intimately.

I no longer suffer from 'vagueness' or an 'ill-defined identity' as far as my standing in Christ is concerned. I know who I am! I am a newly created child of the living God, having been born again and adopted into His family. I have inherited all that belongs to my Heavenly Father, including authority over the enemy. Through the power of the Holy Spirit, who *is* in me, I am well equipped to be victorious in whatever challenges life may bring. I have the means to be more than a conqueror, thanks to my standing and identity in Christ.

I no longer suffer from spiritual 'fatigue' due to constantly striving in my fleshly strength and ability to live up to my expectations as a Christian. The 'blocked mindset' that kept me from moving forward in my spiritual growth, bound to a slave-to-the-flesh mentality, has finally been released and unblocked. I have a clearer understanding of where my source of empowerment comes from. I no longer rely on my fleshly efforts to become the 'pure and lovely Bride' my Heavenly Husband desires. Instead, I rely on the power of the Holy Spirit, who does His working power of sanctification, gradually transforming me, His Bride, into 'The Beauty of Holiness'.

What a blessing to know that I have a Heavenly Husband who *is perfect* in every way. In God, I can have my every need fulfilled. In God, I find a faithful Husband who will never leave me nor forsake me. As I trust Him, I am assured that everything that happens to me in this life will ultimately work together for my good. I can be secure knowing that He loves me intimately. He loves me so much that He was willing to sacrifice His life for me on the Cross, making it possible for me to spend eternity in His loving presence and embrace.

God is in the process of preparing a perfect place for me to dwell with Him forever. Jesus assured His disciples of His impending return from heaven to receive His Bride to Himself in John 14:1-3 with the words:

"Let not your heart be troubled; you believe in God, believe also in Me. In My Father's house are many mansions; if it were not so, I would have told you. I go to prepare a place for you. And if I go and prepare a place for you, I will come again and receive you to Myself; that where I am, there you may be also." (NKJV)

Wow! Imagine that! My Heavenly Husband is in the process of preparing a mansion for me in heaven. The time is coming when He will return to redeem His Bride, to take me to Himself and His eternal kingdom permanently. In the meantime, I need to prepare for His imminent return, which could happen sooner rather than later, and no doubt when we all least expect it.

PART VII

Finally

CHAPTER 22

The Wedding Vow - It's Your Choice

I have come to realise the incredible significance of God's spoken Word. He spoke the universe into being by simply declaring it to be so. My very life depends on God's ever sustaining Word and grace.

Adam and Eve were doomed to death and condemnation because they did not heed God's Word. God had provided for their every need in the perfect Garden of Eden. At the beginning of time, they were living by *faith* in God's provision. All that they needed for life and *fulfilment* had been provided for them through the spoken Word of God. But then came the fall.

God had spoken to Adam and Eve deliberate words of instruction in which He offered them *life* or *death*. The choice came down to either living by *faith*, resulting in life, or living according to their *flesh*, resulting in death. The choice came down to either *heeding* God's voice by *being obedient* to His Word, or *disregarding* God's voice through *disobedience* to His Word. The choice came down to either living *dependent* on God through *faith,* or *independent* of God through self-dependency in the *flesh*.

You and I have before us the very same choice. Do we choose the way of faith that leads to fulfilment and eternal life? Or do we choose the way of the flesh that leads to hopelessness and eternal death and separation from God?

I choose life, and I pray that you do too!

◇◇◇◇◇◇◇◇

When I first sat down to write this book, I really didn't have much of a clue where it was heading or what would end up in its pages. As far as life stories are concerned, I consider mine to be relatively non-eventful when compared to the testimony of others. Nonetheless, it was in obedience to God's leading that I took up the challenge to write down my story thus far.

As I near the end of this quest, I look back and am very much aware that God's hand has been on the pages of my life and the pages of this book. In both cases, the Lord has just kept adding another chapter.

It may well be that you have read my story and are unsure whether you have a ring of engagement on your finger, so to speak. You may not have the assurance that you are betrothed to be married to Jesus, the Heavenly Bridegroom. Is your name written in the Book of Life, on God's marriage certificate, as it were? Do you have assurance of an inheritance in God's eternal Kingdom that He is currently preparing for His betrothed?

The means of acquiring an 'engagement ring' is really very simple. Jesus has proposed His offer of marriage and is longing for you to accept it. In His proposal, He gives you a choice. Do you choose to accept His offer of eternal life spent in His loving presence? Or do you choose eternal death and separation from God?

Jesus has demonstrated how much He loves you. You were on His mind when He laid down His life on the Cross. Jesus is your means of salvation. He is currently waiting at the altar with a wedding ring in hand, offering salvation to all who will come and meet Him there.

All that is required of you is to simply say **'I do'**. Come, just as you are. Come to Jesus and declare to Him your wedding vow by speaking the following words to Him in prayer:

> ***I do** come to You, Jesus, as a sinner, knowing I am incomplete and unrighteous without You. **I do** offer myself to You as Your Bride, knowing it is only in You that I can find forgiveness for my sins and be saved from an eternity without You. **I do** accept Your offer of salvation and marriage, Yourself having laid down Your life for me. **I do** commit my whole life to You as a living sacrifice. **I do** accept You now in faith, giving You honour and glory as the head and founder of my salvation. **I do** thank You, Lord Jesus, that You take me just as*

I am, accepting my hand in marriage to be Your Bride. **I do** *promise to live for You for the rest of my life. In Your name, I pray, Amen.'*

And the best part is that you don't even have to say 'Till death do us part' because not even death can separate you from the love and presence of God if you put your faith in Him.

If you have sincerely prayed this prayer, you are now wearing an engagement ring. It really is that simple. Just as Abraham's servant gave Rebekah gifts of jewellery to indicate that she was Isaac's chosen bride, you have now received God's stamp of approval, the gift of His Spirit as your seal of salvation. You have the assurance that your name is written in God's Book of Life. You can be guaranteed that God has become united with you in the form of His indwelling Holy Spirit. Simply have *faith* in God's Word, believing that what He says in His written Word, the Bible, is the whole truth and nothing but the truth.

Now is the time to get to know your Heavenly Husband. Acquire a hunger to know Him intimately by making the reading of His Word a priority. Acquire a listening ear as He speaks to you with the still small voice of His Holy Spirit. Simply bask in His love, for God *is* Love. Bask *in* Him!

I have finally found the secret to finding fulfilment in my relationship with my Heavenly Husband. I only need to **rest** and **abide**... *in Him.*

Rest - Relax Entirely Submit Totally!

Abide - Always Being In Divine Embrace!

'The Beauty of Holiness' is the expression of God's Grace! Intimacy with God personified!

One... with Him!

References

Murray, A 2003, *Abiding in Christ,* Bethany House Publishers, Bloomington, Minnesota.

Prince, D 1999, *Derek prince on experiencing God's power,* Whitaker House, New Kensington, PA.

Thompson, S 2000, *You may all prophesy,* Morning Star Publications, Fort Mill, SC.

Wilkinson, B 2000, *The prayer of jabez,* Multnomah Publishers, Inc. Sisters, Oregon.

Quotations from Scriptures

Life Application Bible, New International Version, 1991, Co-Published by Tyndale House Publishers, Inc. Wheaton, Illinois, USA and Zondervan Publishing House, Grand Rapids, Michigan, USA.

Scripture quotations marked (AMP) are from the *Large print amplified bible*, 1987, Zondervan Publishing House, Grand Rapids, Michigan, USA.

Scripture quotations marked (NIV) are from the *Thompson Chain-Reference Bible New international version*, 1984, Co-Published by: B.B. Kirkbride Bible Co., Inc Indianapolis, Indiana, USA and The Zondervan Corporation, Grand Rapids, Michigan, USA.

Scripture marked (NKJV) are from the New King James Version. Copyright 1979, 1980, 1982, Thomas Nelson Publishers, Nashville, USA.

PART VIII

A Collection of Song Lyrics and Poems

This was my prayer as I attempted to compose my very first song.

Lord, Give Me a Song

Lord, give me a song that I might sing
just what You mean to me
A song of hope . . . a song of love
that others they may see
The awesome God creator
of the heavens and the earth
Yet you humbled Yourself
that I might live You died a cruel death

You are my hope . . . You are my light
You are my joy . . . You are my life
You are my strength . . . You are my all
You are my God . . . You are my Lord

Lord, give me a song that I might sing
of the miracle of life
How You died for all yet You rose again
victorious You won the fight
The devil's armies flee with fear
they know that they have lost
Lord of all, it was through Your love
You paid the final cost

You are my hope . . . You are my light
You are my joy . . . You are my life
You are my strength . . . You are my all
You are my God . . . You are my Lord

Lord, I pray with all my might
that through me there may be

A reflection of Your holy being
that others they may see
The love You showed for one and all
forgiveness to impart
Now eternal life is given to those
with Jesus in their heart

You are my hope . . . You are my light
You are my joy . . . You are my life
You are my strength . . . You are my all
You are my God . . . You are my Lord

I wrote this song for a friend who lost her husband to cancer at a very young age, leaving her and two young sons.

Take My Hand

One day I stood just gazing
I couldn't help but stare
At the wonders of creation
nothing could compare
God's blessings all around
I know that life's been good to me
But then my heart is troubled
life's misfortunes do I see

Such tragedies and trials
that some are called to bear
I ask myself why is it so
it seems God doesn't care
Then as I stood there gazing
so confused and in despair
I heard a voice . . . I looked around
Jesus was standing there

And He said
seek my face . . . and I will comfort you
Leave all your cares with Me
and I will see you through
My ways are not your ways
someday you'll see
My perfect plan revealed
no more to be concealed
Someday you'll understand
in the meantime take My hand

I have a friend
she loves the Lord
Her faith is strong and sure
One day her faith is tested
she is shattered to the core
She had to ask
How can it be that life is so unfair?
She heard a voice . . . she looked around
Jesus was standing there

And He said
seek my face . . . and I will comfort you
Leave all your cares with Me
and I will see you through
My ways are not your ways
someday you'll see
My perfect plan revealed
no more to be concealed
Someday you'll understand
in the meantime take My hand

This is a song of thanks to my Lord for bearing the burden of my sins.

What More Can I Say

Lord, I seek forgiveness . . . for the sin within my life
It seems that I have lost control . . . I want to do what's right
But time and time again
I find those demons creeping in
Now my heart is burdened
with the shame and guilt of sin

I was just a child . . . when I first gave my heart to You
Now I am reminded . . . what it was You came to do
You sent Your one and only Son
to show how much You care
It was the burden of my sin
Your Son was called to bear

What can I do . . . Hey . . . what can I say
You've taken the burden of my sins away
You sent Your one and only Son
His blood was shed for me
Now I am forgiven . . . yes now I am free
What can I do Lord . . . but give my life to You
What can I say Lord . . . but thank You
What can I do Lord . . . but give my love to You
What more can I say Lord . . . I love You

Now that I have been redeemed
Lord make me more like Thee
Help me shake those demons
that keep taking hold of me
Renew my mind
and fill me with Your Spirit each new day

Guide me Lord
and use me for Your glory this I pray

Sing praise to the Father
sing praise to the Son
My new life with Jesus now
has only begun
Death has been conquered
and now I look forward
To life ever after
with Jesus my Lord
What can I do Lord
but give my life to You
What can I say Lord
but thank You
What can I do Lord
but give my love to You
What more can I say Lord
I love You

What more can I say

The Gospel in a nutshell.

Imagine

Have you ever paused to ponder
on what it was the Lord intended
When He formed the heavens and earth so long ago
It was a paradise of splendour
it was pure perfection rendered
A place where peace and joy and blessings flow

In the Garden of Eden
God created man and women
To dwell with Him in peace and harmony
Yes this was God's intention
until one day man was tempted
He broke God's law when Satan had his way

Imagine . . . can you imagine
How it must have caused His heart to break when the Lord looked down to see
Man turn away and choose to disobey
It was in the Garden of Eden
sin had cost mankind his freedom
Now death's the penalty we're doomed to pay

But that's not where the story ends
God had a plan you see
He sent His one and only Son to die for you and me
He paid the penalty of sin
now eternity we'll spend with Him
If we'll only learn to trust Him and obey

Imagine . . . can you imagine

A world . . . of tranquil peace . . . of joy . . . eternal bliss
Where tears and pain and wars do not exist
Eternal life with God above
where He surrounds us with His love
Yes that's God's plan for every one of us

So will you trust Him as your Lord
He'll guide you on your way
Just seek forgiveness for your sin and walk with Him each day
Then you'll enter heaven's gate
where there is no more sin or hate
When the Lord returns again to take us home

Imagine

Songs of heartfelt praise and worship.

I Give You All the Praise

As I come . . . before You Lord
I marvel at Your majesty and grace
And as I stand . . . in awe of You
I long to know Your touch and see Your smiling face
And for the love You showed to me
And for Your grace that set me free
And for the gift of Your dear Son
I lift Your precious name on high

And I just want to praise You Lord
For the blessings that You've given me
For the privilege of serving You
Through Christ I have the victory
As I shelter beneath Your wings
Of Your mercies I long to sing
As I lift up Your name on high
I give You all the praise

Just a Simple Song of Praise

Lord above the heavens
Creator of all living things
We come before You now oh Lord to sing Your praises
We lift Your precious name on high
We lift our hands towards the sky
As we exalt the King of Kings and Lord of Lords

Just a simple song of praise to You
It is my heart's desire to worship You
To proclaim the Lord my God who saved my soul
Just a simple song of praise to You
It is my heart's desire to live for You
To reflect the life of Christ who made me whole

I wrote this song for a lady I used to work with. I had invited her to a ladies function at church but unfortunately she didn't come. In my disappointment, I wrote this song for her.

Do You Know Him?

Is there something missing in your life
does your soul cry out for more
Does your day seem black as night
an endless empty void
Well I'd like you to meet a friend of mine
for I was feeling just the same
He's made a difference to my life
Jesus is His name

Do you know Him . . . God creator of the world
Do you know Him . . . the one the prophets had foretold
He's the one who gives life meaning
He's the one who makes me whole
He's the one who gave His life to save my soul
Do you know Him . . . as your saviour and your friend
Do you know Him . . . on His love you can depend
How I pray that you will meet Him
Before your time on earth is through
For He loves you and He longs to spend eternity with you

As a child of God I am truly blessed
for I know I need not fear
Whatever troubles life may bring
I have a friend so near
Who will comfort me and keep me
'til my life on earth is through
He fulfils my every need
He'll do the same for you

Do you know Him . . . God creator of the world
Do you know Him . . . the one the prophets had foretold
He's the one who gives life meaning
He's the one who makes me whole
He's the one who gave His life to save my soul
Do you know Him . . . as your saviour and your friend
Do you know Him . . . on His love you can depend
How I pray that you will meet Him
Before your time on earth is through
For He loves you and He longs to spend eternity with you

A poem I wrote for a friend after a difficult year.

Freedom in Strife

As another year comes to a close
I'm sure you would agree
It hasn't been the best of years
that we will ever see
Who would have thought
this time last year
just what we had in store
The trials and the heartache
we've been shattered to the core

At times like these
we tend to ask why
that God would allow all the hurt
For I know that He loves us dearly
but . . . He wants us to stay alert
For when things are going smoothly
we tend to let down our guard
It seems that we only reach out to Him
when life is troubled and hard

I'm sure He hates to see us hurt
His heartache I need not mention
But often distractions clutter our lives
and He needs to get our attention
He wants us to put Him first above all
and so it's such a shame
To think that in order to do this
we must suffer loss and pain

But take heart and be encouraged

for in the Bible we are told
That He chastens those He loves
you and me . . . to shape us and to mould
All I can say after all we've been through
He must love us very much
He longs for us to grow close to Him
to pray and keep in touch

He created us for relationship
to worship Him after all
It stands to reason His anguish
when we seemingly ignore
All that He has done for us
His love and amazing grace
We need to turn our lives around
repent and seek His face

I know that you have suffered much
much more than others it seems
But God above is watching you
His eye is very keen
To see just how you handle it
which path you choose to take
To give up and live defeated
would be a huge mistake

Satan's convinced you he's not involved
I warn you this is his ploy
For when you think it's not his fault
he's won and you are his toy
For he is the king of deception
I know you've been told this before
Whether or not you believe his lies
will determine your future for sure

He wants you to feel defeated and lost
confused as to which way to go
While ever he has a stronghold on you
He's determined to never let go
I've been praying for you constantly

for deliverance from oppression
That you'd be released from this stronghold
of anxiety and depression

Please recognise that Satan's the one
who's causing your life to crumble
Because he knows you belong to God
His aim is to cause you to stumble
So take up the challenge, be victorious
for this is what God has in mind
He conquered all when he sent his Son
to die for all mankind

Choose God, choose life, choose victory
with Him you can conquer all
Choose God's way over Satan's
listen and heed His call
For I know that if you put God first
His blessings will just flow
And as you study and read His word
your spiritual life will grow

Then everything else will fall into place
His will for your life you will see
No more bondage or confusion
you'll be free from anxiety
For its only when we release to Him
our troubles and our needs
And recognise His blood was shed
in order to set us free

That we can experience healing
in all areas of our life
Emotional, spiritual, physical
we'll know liberty and freedom 'in' strife
I say 'in' strife for God never promised
that all would always go well
But as His children He promised us
that if we ever fell

That He would be there to pick us up
and help us when we stray
A faithful God to be our friend
and guide us along the way
And so I pray that God would win
this battle for your mind
And as you meditate on His word
I'm sure that you will find

More clarity in your thinking
no more tossing to and fro
Fill your mind with positive thoughts
God's will for your life you will know
And so I pray with all my heart
that the coming year will bring a new start
That all that you've suffered all anguish will fade
For on the cross your curse was laid

It was laid on Him who suffered your pain
Who died to take your place
He bore your sin. . . your suffering your shame
so relax and rest in His grace
So hand your troubles over to God
no need to do it alone
And just remember you've been redeemed
an heir to God's own throne

He loves you so much. . . just as you are
so learn to love yourself
For you are His . . . a child of God
you even inherit His wealth
So love and be loved this Christmas time
dispel with all your fear
May peace and joy reign in your heart
as you face another new year

Dedicated to my daughter Nimali. This poem was written before she met her husband Matthew

A Mother's Heart for her Daughter

As I ponder anew this Christmas time
the gift of Your dear Son
How Mary . . . just an ordinary girl
was chosen to be Your mum
I am humbled, oh God, that You would choose me
out of all the women in the world
To be the mother of this little one
a beautiful baby girl

I'll never forget that special day
when we met for the very first time
We'd waited so long, yet here she was
this beautiful baby was mine
A tiny little bundle
just wrapped in an old worn towel
Her nappy was nothing but an old torn rag
Her limbs as thin as dowel

Just three weeks later when we brought her home
she filled out very well
She had lots of love and nourishment
but only time would tell
What life would have in store for us
as our baby girl would grow
As life brings joys and turmoil
Her character would show
Sugar and spice and all things nice
or so we had been told
That little girls are made of this
we would see as the years unfold

Sugar and spice, I would agree
a sweetie through and through
To say that she is 'all' things nice
may be telling a tale or two

Still, I love her with all my heart
and do my very best
To nurture and to guide her
and pray God would do the rest
To shape her and to mould her
into the person He'd have her be
My precious daughter is just on lend
she belongs to God you see

He loves her unconditionally
as He would have me do
Though she may not be perfect
she is precious this is true
And one day she will find a man
someone special her life to share
And I as her mother will have to let go
and leave her in his care

For my daughter's future husband
whoever he might be
I pray he too will feel truly blessed
to be chosen just like me
For stability and security
is all she really needs
To know that she is truly loved
in all her human deeds

For my daughter and future husband
whoever he might be
I pray a special blessing
that they would know and see
That putting the other before yourself
is all you need to do
As God showed unconditional love
sacrificial love for you

Just remember through those difficult times
that I can sympathise
Just know that I am praying
that your choices would be wise
It's often the ones we love the most
that are hurt right to the core
Just remember God's unconditional love
and love each other more

How does one begin to express
the depth of our God's love
That He would stoop to this earth below
this King from heaven above
He came as a baby, this King of Kings
destined to die on a cross
For me and for you
sacrificial love . . . with His life He paid the cost

Oh the depth of his unfailing love
that He'd sacrifice Himself
In spite of my imperfections
oh the depth of love that He felt
For me . . . though I am unworthy
though I aim to be all that I can
Because of His unconditional love
He accepted me as I am

And so I pray for my daughter
someone special with whom she can share
All of her life the good and the bad
that together they will bear
The burdens and the trials
that will surely come their way
That they'll love each other warts and all
forever ...come what may

(Thank you, Lord, for Matthew . . . in answer to my prayer)

Dedicated to my son Christopher

Our Beautiful Boy

We waited for you for four long years
from India you would come
You were two years old when you finally arrived
in Australia to be our son
From Sri Lanka God gave us a daughter
a blessing through and through
God had already blessed us with much
and then along came you

When you finally arrived from India
your age being only two
We cannot begin to imagine
just how hard this was for you
You'd been taken away from everything
that you had ever known
For two years in an orphanage
in India you had grown

Two social workers from your home
Had brought you to this land
Too young to know what was happening
you just did not understand
It didn't help that you were asleep
when you arrived you see
And while you slept the social worker
Handed you to me

And when you roused and opened your eyes
you immediately took fright
It seems that you felt that my strange white face

was not a pretty sight
And so it seemed for a very long time
you would look at me and scream
For days you would give me that 'don't touch me' look
it seemed like a really bad dream

But thankfully . . . you took to your Dad
with him for a while you would stay
Like a baby koala you'd cling to him
then finally one day
Your Aunty Janine had had enough
of seeing me so sad
She knew that you needed your Mother
just as much as you needed your Dad

She literally wrenched you away from him
and launched you into my arms
To those who read this it might seem harsh
but my sister had no qualms
For quite frankly she had had enough
a joke it was beyond
She sent us outside just you and me
to take some time to bond

And so it was a special time
as you softened towards your mum
For a very precious moment
you spoke in your mother tongue
Though I did not understand
just what you were trying to say
A mother-and-son relationship
was birthed that special day

Then just when you started to settle
we were finally very relieved
You ended up in hospital with
food poisoning would you believe
You were limp and almost lifeless
we were feeling very afraid
But God came through and answered our prayers

from death you had been saved

Our beautiful boy from India
in stature you are small
But in good looks and character
you stand up ten feet tall
For if these special attributes
were an indication of size
In a 'good looks' and 'character' contest
you would surely win the prize

Your humour is contagious
I'm sure all would agree
The stories and tales you tell so well
make us laugh and tickle our fancy
Your SMS texts would indicate
that 'your' fancy is tickled as well
For every second word you write
is followed by LOL

You've grown into a fine young man
a carpenter you would become
You worked the same trade both you and your Dad
as Jesus God's own Son
It is our prayer your Father and I
that in Jesus steps you would tread
In every area of your life
by His Holy Spirit be lead

We believe God brought you here to us
for this very purpose you see
Not just to become 'our' own dear son
to be part of 'our' family
But more importantly than that
God loves you very much
He longed for you to become 'His' son
yes even more than us

He brought you here from India
for this very purpose you see

He knew that we would pass on to you
our family legacy
For down through the generations
our parents have passed on God's word
And through His Holy Bible
His love for us we have heard

He adopts us into His family
We only need to believe
And give our lives completely to Him
through Jesus we've been redeemed
And so we entrust you to God's care
And pray for you every day
And praise Him for the blessing you've been
to us in every way

A poem dedicated to my Dad.

Where do I start to express from my heart
the words that I want to say
To a Dad who was broken and weak and worn
as on your bed you would lay

A Dad . . . My Dad, who all your life
Has sought to honour the Lord
A quiet gentle spirit was yours
and by many you were loved and adored

You were highly respected by all that you knew
a gentleman through and through
A man of many talents you were
though humbly. . . you would hide them from view

Like your gift of playing the piano
for many a tune you could play
Though you tended to think you weren't good enough
your talents to put on display

Your gift of writing poetry
is one that is known by few
And much to Mum's embarrassment
you told a tale or two

Like the time that in your caravan
in the middle of the night
That thing's became quite desperate it seems
as Mum floundered to turn on the light

An accident was imminent
as her bladder was carrying a load
You told the tale in a poem called
'The PORTALOO EPISODE'

I loved the way when I was young
when I couldn't go to sleep
You would play your guitar and sing to me
a melody so sweet

And if that didn't work, you would sit for a while
for as long as it would take
And stroke me on my forehead until
I slept. . . no longer awake

As a young man you were agile
a specimen of health and fitness
Your sporting prowess was to be admired
by all who would see and witness

You could turn your hand to any sport
be it tennis or bowls or golf
You could run like the wind
you could dart here and there
like a horse at the gate you would bolt.

Your love of sport you passed to us girls
your skills you'd endeavour to teach
I will always have very fond memories of watching you hop
skip. . . and jump on the beach

We shared your love of hockey too
and high jump. . . though it was hard
You set up two poles and a beam for us girls
to practice in the backyard

In later years things took their toll
and your body began to break down
Yet still in your typical unselfish way
you would never complain or frown

I cannot begin to understand
the pain that you went through
Or why you had to suffer so much more
than you were due

There was nothing I could do or say
to take your pain away
But Christ had suffered
He knew your pain
and so to Him I would pray

For you taught us from a very young age
to put our trust in Him
And God who is faithful would see us through
when life is hard and grim

You taught us too
from God's Holy word
that Christ died that we might live
Upon Himself He took our death
His life to us He gives

And so by faith we believe it's true
and though your body decays
Your soul and spirit have flown and live on
in heaven for everlasting days

And so through the generations
we will pass on this legacy
That as Christians God's Spirit
lives within . . . a mystery that is Christ in me

So for those of you who knew my Dad
and wondered just what it could be
That caused him to be such a wonderful man
it was God's reflection you could see

So thank you for giving us Jesus
Dad . . . it was the best thing you could do

For when our time on this earth is done
we will end up in heaven with you

So though we are sad and will miss you for sure
and life will not be the same
We look forward to the time on that heavenly shore
when we all get to see you again

We love you, beautiful Daddy!

As a testament to my much-loved Dad, I have dedicated this book to his memory. What better way to honour my dear Dad and my heavenly Father both, than by concluding with Dad's hand-written testimony declaring his devotion and adoration for his Saviour and Lord.

HAND-WRITTEN PERSONAL TESTIMONY OF DONALD ROYCE McKEOUGH

My Dad!

I have known about Jesus Christ for as long as I can remember. At the age of 12 I met Him personally. At that time I realised that I was a sinner, that I had been tried and found guilty, and that the sentence of death had been passed upon me. I knew that of myself there was nothing I could do to retrieve the situation. I seemed doomed for eternity. But Jesus saw my plight and obviously felt a great deal towards me. The guilt and sentence that was mine He chose to take upon Himself, and He died in my place, the just for the unjust, thereby proving His great love for me.

Now I'm free. Free, of the guilt that bound me, free to serve Jesus as my Saviour and Lord, free to face the future with the assurance of life eternal. I can only recommend Him as being the most patient, most forgiving, most loving and most sustaining person I have ever known and the only one to whom you can go for salvation for He said, "No man cometh unto the Father but by me." Peter said of Him in Acts 4-12. "Neither is salvation found in any other: for there is none other name under heaven, given among men whereby we must be saved." To any who do not know Him as Saviour I would urge you in the words of the Psalmist. "O taste & see that the Lord is good. Blessed is the man that trusteth in Him."

About the Author

Sharon Longworth has had a PhD attached to her name for over forty-five years. Her field of expertise being… **P**rofessional **h**air-**D**ressing…! That's right! Sharon has no claim whatsoever to academic accolades and is content to admit to such. She had therefore given little consideration over the years to the possibility of becoming an author. Nonetheless, God, in His mysterious ways, assigned Sharon the task of writing this book. His persuasive means allowed her little resistance to refuse the challenge.

Sharon and her husband Andrew are blessed with two adopted children, now adults. Nimali was born in Sri Lanka and Christopher in India. They have a wonderful son-in-law Matthew, and two precious grandchildren, Thomas Royce and Minnie Grace.

Sharon and Andrew are self-employed business owners in the hairdressing and building trades. They reside on the beautiful Mid North Coast of NSW, Australia.

Contact the author: author.sharonlongworth@gmail.com

www.ingramcontent.com/pod-product-compliance
Lightning Source LLC
Chambersburg PA
CBHW071300110526
44591CB00010B/724